# How to
# Hike, Camp and
# Backpack

Roger H. Meyer

# How to Hike, Camp and Backpack

## DEDICATION

This book is dedicated to the men and women who enjoy the outdoors and think everyone should do so.

The outdoors provides enjoyment, exercise and mental improvement. Being outdoors improves mind and body. It gets you away from the hustle of our modern culture and helps maintain a sense of calmness and tranquility.

There's a lot to learn about the outdoors and this book is a start. Bring your children along also. I'll never forget the expression on my son's face the first time we encountered a deer in the woods. Enjoy.

Roger Meyer

i

# CONTENTS

# Healthy Walking

This a different spin on walking. Most people know of the health reasons to walk. This book will emphasize the enjoyable aspects and the non-health related rewards of walking.

This book will not say "See your doctor before starting this exercise program" or "Buy a good pair of walking shoes." You don't need to be told this.

Items covered by this book will include: how to vary your walk so it never becomes dull and repetitive, what to look for and at as you walk, and activities while you walk. Walking can be interesting and enjoyable, in addition to being beneficial and low cost. Acquire mental and physical benefits with minimal effort and sweat and no aches or pains. There's not much risk of injury or damage to joints.

This book will dispel the common "Do I have to walk?" attitude. "A Fun Way to Exercise" presents new attributes of walking.

This exercise also improves your mental processes (many creative people do it) and gently relaxes your body. It allows time for thought and contemplation.

If you say exercise is enjoyable, you're fooling yourself. Do you really enjoy the sweat, the time involved, or the occasional aches and pains?

What most people really like is the result of that physical activity. They might like the way they feel after a workout, or their improved appearance with an exercise program, or maybe they just want to live longer. Everyone discovers they feel better, sleep better, stay fit and trim, and are happier. But, sometimes I bet they wish they could eliminate the sweat and the discomfort.

What would you say to an enjoyable exercise program? One that's interesting, beneficial, and low cost. The effort and the sweat are minimal without aches and pains. There's little risk of injury or damage to joints. No special equipment or scheduled time commitments. You even can complete errands while exercising.

This exercise also improves your mental processes (many creative people do it) and gently relaxes your body. It allows time for
thought and contemplation. Would you be surprised that it's also the most popular exercise? There's one problem, you may need to revamp your opinion of this activity, because some people think it's wimpy.

Of course, our miraculous exercise is walking. "Do You Know Why Walking is the Most Popular Exercise?" allows your readers to take another look at the wonderful benefits of walking..

# Enjoy Your Exercise

Do not even think about jogging. Walk instead. Walking provides physical conditioning with little chance for injuries or the physical problems often caused by jogging. Walking is inexpensive and can be combined with other activities and hobbies.

The Massai, an African tribe, exist on a high fat and cholesterol diet. Their food is almost entirely meat and milk. But, as a group, they have the lowest documented incidence of heart problems in the world. The explanation for this apparent paradox is simple. They walk a minimum of ten miles a day tending their cattle. The physical and mental benefits of walking allow an elderly Massai to have the same blood pressure as a teenager.

Walking reduces blood pressure, keeps you fit and trim, reduces the effects of osteoporosis, helps you live longer, lowers stress levels, and isn't limited to a particular season. Almost anybody can walk.

Talk to a jogger. Many will mention painful shin splints, being chased by dogs, the need to push to do their miles, and so on. Then, talk to a walker. They will tell you about the enjoyment walking brings them.

After you have your doctor's permission and begin to increase your walking capabilities, you will want to go on longer and longer hikes. Then, you have joined the wonderful world of day hikers.

A day hike can be a memorable walk. You can hike on sidewalks, beaches, roads, or trails. You can hike alone or with others, and you can hike with your parents or your grandchildren.

Go for a few hours or a few days. A day hike can be combined with other activities, such as photography, treasure hunting, sightseeing, bird watching, and all kinds of nature study.

To introduce your family to nature, take a day hike away from a city. Recently, I spent an enjoyable afternoon with my children. During an eight-mile walk along a forest trail, we spent time watching a pair of turtles and about 20 minutes taking pictures of a raccoon family. A hawk seized a rabbit about thirty feet from us while we sat quietly resting, and we flushed two deer after approaching within about 50 feet of them. We spotted an owl in a tree and identified it with a bird book. A grove of trees was teeming with squirrels and we enjoyed watching their antics. We spent a few solemn moments near the corpse of a doe. She became tangled in a wire fence and starved to death.

We stopped and looked whenever we saw something interesting. The eight-mile hike took close to five hours, so we weren't trying to break a speed record. Our observations and experiences on this hike will be with us for a long time.

Day hikes in the city are also worthwhile. You may discover unique shops or great ideas for decorating and landscaping as you look at other homes. Close observation of sights that you zoom pass in a car will make the scenery come alive and you will gain insight into your community.

In a city, pick a mall, library, or a fast food restaurant as a destination. It can provide refreshments, toilets, and a place to sit and rest before you return home. Consider how to return to your starting point. You could walk, but this means you must select a loop or retrace your path. You could arrange for someone to pick you up at your destination, but if your driver is not familiar with the pickup spot, take care to avoid a misunderstanding. A phone call after arriving at your destination works fine. Public transportation works for some hikers.

I know one person who parks his car at the destination, then cycles to a starting point and then drives back to the bicycle after walking. If you hike with others, try spotting their car at the destination and driving back to the starting point in your car.

Allow one-half hour for each mile plus time for lunch, rest stops, and sightseeing. You might walk at a faster pace, but this is a good guideline at first. Allow another half-hour for each 1000° feet on an ascent or descent along your route. After some conditioning, many hikers are able to increase their walking speed to three, or even four, miles per hour.

Every day hiker should carry a few items. A city hiker does not need as much as a trail hiker because things like water and food are often available alone the route and a city hiker can call a taxi if a problem develops. Carry a few items on all hikes, moleskin, map, compass, and change for a phone call. Moleskin is a felt-like adhesive material found in the foot care department of drug stores. It will prevent blisters if used at the first sign of discomfort. A map     and compass are desirable because anyone can become confused and lost, even in a city.

Depending on the route and length of your hike, food, water, emergency items, extra clothing, or rain gear should be taken on your hike. Some hikers carry a camera, binoculars, a walking stick, fishing gear, books to read, or guidebooks for nature study, and other individual items. If your hike takes you away from civilization, prepare yourself with appropriate emergency items. You should consider a first aid kit, insect repellent, sun tan lotion, matches, a space blanket, whistle, snake bite kit, knife, flashlight, toilet paper, and a trowel. The trowel is used to bury body wastes.

The sound of a whistle will carry farther than shouting if you need help. A space blanket is aluminum foil supported by flexible plastic layers and folds up to about the size of a deck of cards. Wrap it around your body for warmth; it reflects about eighty percent of your radiated heat back towards your body and can serve as an emergency shelter. It costs only a few dollars.

Some of the items are for emergencies or for unplanned overnight campouts. A twisted ankle, a fall, or getting lost may force you to make camp after sunset. If only a few items are carried, use pockets or a belt pouch. Use a musette bag, fanny pack, or a small daypack for more items. I prefer a musette bag (often called a messenger bag) because it allows easier access to a camera or binoculars than the other carriers.

Some day hikers wear hiking boots, but comfortable shoes or sneakers are OK. Boots become more desirable if you intend to carry a heavy load, to hike rough trails, or to hike for several consecutive days. Ankles need the support provided by boots when hiking under these conditions.

Dress in layers rather than wearing a heavy jacket and adjust the number of layers for comfort. Several light layers provide more warmth and protection than one heavy garment and weighs less.

A few people like to day hike for several days in a row. They sleep in motels or hotels. Of course, these hikes require more planning. You do not want to hike to the only motel for ten miles in any direction and discover it's full. I heard of a man who hiked from Boston to New York City using this method.

If you plan to hike for several days, consider eating at least two meals a day in restaurants. Perhaps for lunch, buy supplies from a supermarket and prepare a trail lunch. Or carry food for light lunches on the trail from home. Some hikers carry a small backpacking stove to heat soup for lunch. Hiking for several days means carrying extra clothing and toilet articles in a small pack. Many Europeans enjoy this kind of hiking. They often use public transportation to return home.

Staying in motels eliminates the burden of a tent, sleeping bag, a large supply of food, and other heavy overnight gear. So, a day hike can be more enjoyable for some of us than a backpacking trip. On backpacking trips, you must tolerate and cope with bad weather. If the weather turns sour on a day hike, you have more options to avoid it.

Your first day hike should be short. Don't overdo it. If you're in reasonable shape, plan a five-mile hike the first time. Plan longer hikes after you know that five miles are comfortable. Work up to about forty miles a day if that suits you, but anything more than fifteen or twenty miles a day means you're not taking much time to smell the flowers. And that should be important to everyone.

Sure, you can find faster and more efficient ways to exercise, but none are as much fun or as much pleasure as the wonderful world of day hiking.

# Things to Carry on a Dayhike

Consider these items:
Daypacks should have capacity for photography equipment or fishing or whatever your hobby is,
food and water - Many day hikers under estimate how much fuel they'll need for 12 to 16 hour pack two lunches plus a few snacks, check water availability, carry more in hot weather, water treatment- a bottle of iodine tablets or other chemical treatment adds very little to your pack
headlamp - if you expect to be out past dark. pack extra batteries, a basic first aid kit a few bandages to antiseptic wife's and some butterfly bandages a triangular manage,
mapping and compass. don't take navigation for granted just because his only a day hike,
a rain shell a light weight shell is ideal. A poncho also works, emergency shelter  - such as a bivy sack or a space blanket or a waterproof rainsuit,
a warm hat - it doesn't take much space to provide warmth,
also considers sunscreen, insect repellent, a whistle and sunglasses.

# TRAIL MAGIC

Do you walk just for exercise? Walkers often move rapidly along with their heads down and their arms pumping away. All they are doing is exercising - which is fine, but there's more to traveling afoot.

A friend criticized my choice of walking for exercise. He said it was so slow that it was boring to him. He said he preferred to either peddle a bike or jog for exercise. Ever watch a biker or jogger? For safety reasons, they must watch their path and seldom see any of the terrain they pass through. Here are some of the things they miss.

I find things as I hike along and often it's money. An unusual acquisition was a $5 gold piece while strolling in a park. It wasn't buried, just lying there in plain sight after a rainstorm.

Another unusual find occurred while dayhiking with a group on a woodland trail in Michigan about three miles from the nearest road. Two of us got a little ahead of the rest of the hikers and we stopped to let them catch up. I leaned against a tree and spotted something shiny on the ground partly covered by leaves. It turned out to be two Israeli coins. Would you ever expect to find those coins where I did?

I read somewhere in an article or book, an author mentioned finding between $3 and $4 a year on her urban hikes. I kept track for a while and sure enough I also retrieved between $3 and $4 a year.

Where snow covers the ground for part of the year, you might find less. It was so repeatable that I knew I needed to walk more if I found less than about 30 cents a month. I encounter coins everywhere, along roadsides, in store parking lots, and on trails in the deep woods. I haven't a clue how they all get there.

You will see many pennies, sometimes a bunch in one area. There's an equal number of dimes and quarters, only occasionally a nickel, and never half-dollars. Occasionally, I'll find paper money; once $15 all folded up. Once I found a $100 bill in a park. I found out later that the park was a spot known for drug deals.

Money isn't the only item found. You'll buy few bolts or nuts, because you see so many. Most of them are obviously from cars. I wonder what fell off after the bolts came out. Or what happened to the wheel after the lug nuts I find came off?

If you chose to, you will never buy another comb. I also picked up a pocketknife, a watch, and a camera (none were very expensive). Several pairs of sunglasses came in handy. I found sunglasses partly buried in a creek bed; it's now my favorite pair.

Once, it was ballpoint pen day. During a 7-mile urban hike, I retrieved nine pens; eight of them worked.

Other items rescued during hikes were butane lighters, golf balls, a neat paint scraper, an ashtray, cups, and a canteen. Even an unopened can of beer and a bottle of Pepsi.

On a road near the seashore in Georgia, I discovered many sharks' teeth. The gravel-like material used to make that road was dredged from the bottom of the bay. The shark's teeth were in that material. I also found a large arrowhead on that road. It was probably on a fishing spear long ago. You'll find an occasional arrowhead on woodland trails also.

I find clothing including T-shirts, sweatshirts, and sweat pants while hiking. People apparently remove them when they get warm, tie them onto their packs, and they accidentally fall off later. I also see jackets and hats left usually at good resting spots. I've rescued several baseball hats while wandering along a shoreline. Probably the wind blew them into the water and they eventually washed up on the shore.

The most unusual find of apparel was in a wilderness area about 500 miles from home where I spotted a pile of clothing left at a scenic view. It included a jacket made for employees of the company I worked for. Unique initials inked inside on the label identified the owner as a co-worker. He was surprised when I was able to return it.

You'll encounter natural items also. You'll see wonderful wildflowers and herbs, morels, and mushrooms. Once, a thousand miles from the ocean I found a seashell.

My kids and I spent a half-hour watching and laughing at the antics of a group of squirrels. A raccoon family played peep-a-boo with us for a while. We watched a pair of ducks mating. It was an introduction to the birds and bees. Later, we passed the carcass of a deer that died after becoming entangled in a wire fence.

If you hike in the woods, you will occasionally surprise deer. The fawns tend to curiously look you over before darting away. Apparently, their fear of humans is acquired as they mature. A hawk grabbed a rabbit about fifteen feet away as we sat quietly resting alongside the trail.

I see many birds as I walk. Bikers and joggers seldom see any wildlife.

On an urban walk, I observed an unexpected miniature-car competition in an empty lot and watched a group fly model planes and rockets from a field. People I met while hiking taught me how to rappel down a cliff and another person taught me how to throw a boomerang. I spotted a person photographing wildflowers. We chatted and he pointed out a variety of the tiny flowers and a great technique for photos. It sparked my interest enough to start a new hobby of photographing them.

A friend and I knew there were only four other people on a 15,000-acre wilderness island. We were dayhiking from a basecamp and we encountered two of those four people going in the opposite direction. We stopped, chatted for a while, and continued on our way. About 10 minutes later, the other pair of hikers came strolling down the trail. They had not seen the first pair of hikers. The odds of all of us hiking the same trail at the same time are astronomical. Long distance hikers might call this "trail magic."

Try traveling around your neighborhood on foot. You'll see things you can't see while driving. I've found shortcuts between streets, inspected new houses, and chatted with the builders. The ruins of an abandoned railroad bridge prompted me to investigate its history. I found several previously unknown nature paths in local parks, some with pretty streams.

I see friends while walking; often they were driving by and stop to chat with me. Occasionally, I encounter events that were embarrassing to others. While hiking in remote areas of parks, I unintentionally interrupt amorous activities. There were a few moments of frantic movement as the participants scrambled to get dressed. Another time, the couple was so preoccupied, they never saw me as I passed quietly within 50 feet. I really tried to look the other way.

One of the items I occasionally see on my walks is underwear, both male and female. I think I know how it gets there.

It's a small world. I crossed a busy street and passed an old man as he hobbled slowly across the intersection. His steps were about 4 inches long and his slow progress held up traffic. I then hiked about seven miles around the city over the next three hours or so. I returned home and at that same intersection, guess who was crossing going the other way. Yep, same man.

I strolled through a zoo and saw a group of bikers decked out in black leather jackets and boots. We said "Hi" to each other. Later that day, while walking along a street about 20 miles away, there they were. "Hi" again.

I chatted briefly with a man in the next seat on a flight to Tampa. Next day while strolling through a parking lot 50 miles away from the airport, guess who? We both did a double take.

Strolling on an urban sidewalk, a car pulled up alongside and the passenger held a furry bundle out the window and yelled, "Want a puppy?"

Hiking in the woods, I encountered a mountain biker who had crashed into a tree. I gave him first aid and got a rescue unit to help him.

Walking is more than stomping along with your head down and arms pumping away. It can be fun and an adventure.

Observe things while walking and you will enrich yourself. Start by trying to discover one new thing every time you leave the house. You'll see more and you'll decorate your life.

# TRAILS ON YOUR DOORSTEP

Why is a trail network important? If you're a hiker, a bicyclist, or a nature lover, you already know. You'll love nature and America more by traveling through it and by getting closer to it. A trail network will become part of our heritage and something your grandchildren will pass along to their grandchildren.

There's more. Our society promotes sedentary lifestyles. With increased use of cars, remote controls, and other labor saving devices Americans are overweight and prone to associated health concerns, included heart problems, diabetes, osteoporosis, and more. Only 10 percent of school children walk to school. Overweight children doubled in numbers in the last 25 years.

The Surgeon General partly blames our health problems on communities having fewer sidewalks and bikeways which increase the use of automobiles.

In 1988, sixteen members of a non-profit coalition called American Trails began a study in cooperation with the National Park Service. The task force released a report, called "Trails For All Americans", that reaches for an ambitious goal - to provide a trail within 15 minutes of every American. The report shows how a nationwide trail will benefit everyone. From increased real estate values to ecosystems to protecting our heritage to exercise, our trail system will rejuvenate America's spirit and health.

In Michigan, Risa Wilkerson of the Governor's Council for Physical Fitness, Health, and sports and Karen Petersmarck of the Michigan Department of Community Health have just created an award to communities that promote transportation by physical activity.

Imagine a person starting on a local trail, moving to a county trail, then to a state trail, and finally a federal trail - and then returning to their departure point without retracing their steps. Everyone has heard of some of our National trails, the Appalachian Trail and the Iditarod. Have you ever heard of the Schockaloe or the Silver Moccasin Trail? These four, along with about 800 more, are part of the present National Trail System.

The National Trails System Act of l968 is intended to develop and protect a system of nationwide trails. The original Act authorized three categories of trails: National Scenic, National Recreation, and Connecting or Side Trails. A 1978 amendment added another category - National Historic Trails.

Trails in two of the categories are established by Act of Congress: National Scenic and National Historic Trails. National Scenic Trails are more than 100 miles long and are primarily non-motorized pathways of special recreation opportunity. National Historic Trails commemorate historic (and prehistoric) travels routes of National significance. They must meet all three criteria listed in Section 5(b)(11) of the National Trails System Act. National Recreation Trails are existing regional and local trails recognized by either the Secretary of Agriculture or the Secretary of the Interior.

Since 1993, we have celebrated the anniversary of the National Trails System Act on the first Saturday in June with National Trails Day. Over 2,000 activities take place every year ranging from fund raising Bar-B-Qs by local hiking clubs, to Boy Scouts on wilderness hikes, to a trail picnic of hikers and mountain bikers together to understand the other group better.

"After many years of effort, the vision that brought about the National Trails Act hasn't been reached, " says Tom Ross, Chief - National Trails and Recreation Branch of the National Park Service. "The challenge for the next 25 years is to finish this vision for all Americans."

But, this will not be easy. Barbara Nelson-Jameson, Midwest Region Outdoor Recreation Planner for the National Park Service says, "We can't do it alone, the public must be involved in this effort."

The public is already involved. According to Susan Henley, Executive Director of the American Hiking Society, there are over 400 organizations involved in some aspect of the trail system. "Most of these organizations use volunteers to create or maintain trails. America has 300,000 miles of trails today. We expect to have at least three to four times that amount in the future."

Of the eight National Scenic Trails authorized by Congress, only the Appalachian Trail and the Pacific Crest Trail can be hiked from end to end. The others are only partly complete.

There's another potential scenic pathway called the American Discovery Trail, which could become the nation's first coast-to-coast footpath from Point Reyes, California to Cape Henlopen State Park, Delaware. In 1991, a scouting team has completed a 14-month journey walking or biking along the entire 4,820 mile proposed pathway.

Ten trails, also authorized by Congress, are designated National Historic Trails. They include the Iditarod, the Santa Fe, the Pony Express, and Mormon Pioneer. Now, they're mostly just plans since only 10% of the total mileage is complete.

The 780 National Recreation Trails range from a short path connecting a parking lot to a scenic waterfall to a 213-mile trail in Kentucky with a nationwide mileage of about 8,400 miles.

Some recreation trails are black-topped and some are waterways. Some are intended for skiers, others for motorcyclists, nature lovers, and horse riders. Every state has at least one.

Many volunteers work on our trails. For example, 4,500 people spend 200,000 hours annually maintaining the 2,150 mile-long Appalachian Trail. The AT is well established and doesn't need as much labor as new trails where the work is just beginning. Through out the United States, volunteers spend almost 600,000 hours working on trails; the estimate value of this labor is almost $9 million.

"Of course, there's a physical health aspect to our trail system," says Henley, "And there's also a mental health benefit that most people don't consider at first. Traveling on a trail is pleasant and relaxing."

Henley adds, "Somebody who doesn't care about their own well-being is not going to get involved with any trail effort, but everyone else might help."

Trails contribute to everyone's health and fitness. They allow an alternate travel route away from all the hazards of motor vehicles; they help protect out natural resources, increase regional tourism, and educate us about our environment.

Many people use trails already. Today:

93 million people bicycle
41 million day hike
10 million ride horses on trails

19

5 million backpack

11 million cross-country ski

43 million are campers, nature photographers, or students of nature.

The number of trail users is increasing. For example, in 1960 only 12 million people were bicyclists and in the next decade backpacking and dayhiking is expected to more than double.

"The next time you're irritated by traffic and feel must be a better way - you're right," says Dave Lillard. "And we think that better way is a compete National Trails Network."

# THREADS OF GREEN

President Johnson said: "We can and should have an abundance of trails for walking, cycling, and horseback riding, in and close to our cities. In the backcountry we need to copy the great Appalachian Trail in all parts of America."

"This need for trails as well as other types of recreation facilities was clearly visible in the post-war boom in recreation participation," says Thomas L. Gilbert, the Midwest Region Coordinator for the National Trail System. "In a survey conducted in 1960 for the Outdoor Recreation Resources Review Commission, created to assess this need, walking for pleasure ranked second among all recreation activities."

The National Trails System Act of 1968 was designed to develop and protect this system of pathways. The original act authorized National Scenic and National Recreation Trails. A 1978 amendment added another category - National Historic Trails.

National Recreation Trails are existing regional and local paths approved by either the Secretary of Agriculture or the Secretary of the Interior. Congress authorizes the other two categories, the National Scenic and National Historic Trails.

To be a National Scenic Trail, the pathway must be more than 100 miles long and intended primarily for non-motorized recreation. National Historic Trails commemorate historic travel routes. They preserve stories of our country's past and they are monuments to America's struggles and bravery.

In 1988, the President's Commission on Americans Outdoors recommended a nationwide network of trails that would "tie this country together with threads of green." They envisioned hikers, joggers, bikers, and equestrians using these pathways.

Later that year, a non-profit coalition called American Trails began a study with the National Park Service. They created a task force which released a report titled Trails For All Americans that reached for an ambitious goal - to provide a footpath within 15 minutes of the home and workplace of most Americans.

Imagine a person starting on a local trail, moving to a county trail, then to a state trail, and finally a federal trail and traveling to anywhere in the country - and then returning to their departure point without retracing their steps. Our national system is something we can pass along to our grandchildren, and then they can pass it along to their grandchildren.

The task force report shows how a nationwide trail system is beneficial to everyone. They said from increased real estate values to exercise to improved ecosystems to protecting our heritage - a trail system will rejuvenate America's spirit and health.

Today, state and local governments are building more trails. Jay Cravens, Manager of Michigan's Cascade Township, says their local paths are featured in real estate ads and a recent tax for township pathways passed easily.

In her successful campaign for governor of Michigan, Jennifer Granholm said, "Bicycle paths and trails provide cherished recreational outlets for Michigan's families. I will work with state and local groups to increase the number of bike paths and trails."

Of the eight National Scenic Trails authorized by Congress, only the Appalachian Trail and the Pacific Crest Trail can be hiked from end to end. The others are only partly finished. For example, the North Country National Scenic Trail is only 40 percent complete.

There's another potential scenic pathway called the American Discovery Trail, which is tentatively planned from Point Reyes, California to Cape Henlopen State Park, Delaware. It could become our first coast-to-coast pathway. In 1991, a scouting team completed a 14-month journey walking or biking along the entire 4,820 mile proposed route.

Fourteen trails are designated National Historic Trails. They include the Iditarod, the Santa Fe, the Pony Express, and Mormon Pioneer Trails. Now, they're mostly planned pathways since only 10 percent of the total mileage is complete.

In June 1971, the first 29 pathways were entered onto the list of National Recreation Trails. Now the list has grown to over 900 trails ranging from a 0.1-mile path in Tennessee to the 410-mile Grand Army of the Republic Highway in Pennsylvania.

Some recreation trails are blacktopped and some are waterways. Some are intended for cross-country skiers, others for motorcyclists, nature lovers, or horse riders. Every state has at least one and 108 are less than one mile long.

In 1993, we started celebrating the anniversary of the National Trails System Act. Since then, the first Saturday in June has been designated National Trails Day. Over 2,000 activities take place during this celebration ranging from fund raising Bar-B-Qs by local hiking clubs to Boy Scouts on wilderness hikes to a picnic with hikers and mountain bikers together to understand the other group better.

Our goal for the future is to finish this vision for all Americans. Even after many years of effort, the dream of Trails For All Americans hasn't been reached. The primary problem, of course, is money.

It's going to be a long and expensive project or series of projects. For example, the Appalachian Trail cost $180 million and took 70 years to complete. And compared to some of the other unfinished national trails: the AT is shorter, more of it is on public land, and it goes through less populated areas.

So, this will not be easy. Barbara Nelson-Jameson, Midwest Region Outdoor Recreation Planner for the National Park Service says, "We can't do it alone, the public must be involved in this effort."

Bob Papp, former Executive Director of The North Country National Trail Association, said, "We've completed more than 1600 miles of the trail. Surprisingly, though, very few people have heard of the 'NCT' or know what it is. We've been at this for twenty years now, but we're reaching a threshold where the hardest segments to build are still ahead. To complete the trail, we'll need to tremendously increase our level of public awareness and support."

Many volunteers are already involved to some degree. Throughout the United States, volunteers spend almost 600,000 hours annually working on our national trails; the estimated value of this labor is almost $9 million.

For example, 4,500 people spend 200,000 hours each year maintaining the Appalachian Trail. The AT is well established and doesn't need as much labor as the new trails where the work is just beginning.

The effort needed for new trails includes the actual construction plus negotiating with landowners for permission for

23

the path to cross their land. Construction includes marking the trail, clearing the pathway of fallen trees, and building boardwalks and bridges in wet areas or across streams.

There are over 400 organizations involved in some aspect of the trail system, Most of these organizations use volunteers to create or maintain trails. America has 300,000 miles of trails today. In the future, we expect to have at least three to four times that amount.

There's also a physical health aspect to the trail system. Most people don't consider this. Traveling on a trail is pleasant and relaxing.

Our society promotes sedentary lifestyles. With the increased use of labor saving devices Americans are fat and getting fatter. Only 10 percent of children walk to school. The number of overweight children has doubled in the last 25 years.

Being overweight leads to health concerns, including heart problems, diabetes and more. The Surgeon General partly blames our health problems on the increased use of automobiles and encourages communities to build more sidewalks and bikeways to increase physical non-motorized activity.

Trails contribute to everyone's health and fitness. They allow an alternate travel routes away from all the hazards of motor vehicles, help protect our natural resources, make us aware of our heritage, increase regional tourism, and educate us about our environment. In 2001, a survey by the Travel Industry Association of America showed than one in four travelers go hiking or bike riding during their travels.

With the passage of the National Trails System Act, we began one of the most significant recreation endeavors in history. No other country in the world has a trail system as extensive, or with as much diversity, as that found in the United States.

According to the American Hiking Society: 155 million Americans walk for pleasure,93 million bicycle, 41 million day hike, 10 million ride horses on trails, 5 million backpack, 11 million cross-country ski,43 million are campers, nature photographers, or students of nature. The number of trail users increases every year and is expected to continue to multiply. For example, in 1960, only 12 million people were bicyclists and in the next decade backpacking and day hiking is expected to more than double.

# Family Fun

Is your family going on vacation to an amusement park again? Are you really looking forward to this? The crowds and the high cost change your family vacation into an irritating and expensive hassle. This year do something different to enrich your family. Go camping.

If you're interested in exploring nature or looking for a low-cost, fun-filled activity, or want a intimate family adventure, go camping. If you want either a relaxing vacation or one filled with challenges, go camping.

Camping offers pleasure and recreation to everyone and more families are camping than ever before. Camping moves families closer to nature and closer to each other. Campers leave the ordinary vacation and commonplace weekend trips to others. Go camping.

Some families camp on only on vacation, others only on weekends, a few camp at every opportunity all year round, and some camp just for a night or two while traveling or sightseeing. Many families use their campsite as a basecamp and then drive to nearby attractions. So, you can even visit an amusement park if your kids have withdrawal pains.

Camping can be more than just camping. Combining it with other activities, such as nature study, photography, exploring, and treasure hunting. Develop an interest in birdwatching or animal tracking. Many campgrounds are near water to allow an opportunity to fish and swim. Play a day hike.

Children and fathers love camping, but mothers sometimes feel differently. Often mothers grow to dislike camping because their workload increases compared to everyday life. To avoid this overload, let the family share the work.

Everyone shares with the chores. Let two people, perhaps an adult and a youngster, work as a team to prepare and cleanup each meal. It teaches teamwork and responsibility. Remember, it's a family activity and the theme is "family camping." Everyone participates and everyone contributes. Let your children plan some meals and activities. Let them participate from the initial plans to final cleanup.

My 16-year-old son recently talked about one of our first family campouts, 12 years ago. He remembered the number of the campsite and the ghost story I told while we sat wrapped in a blanket together on a chilly evening by the campfire. I knew my children enjoyed camping, but I didn't realize it created such lasting memories.

Like anything else, camping is easier if you know what you're doing. Everything's a little smoother with an experienced person along on your first campout, but it's not really necessary. You can handle it alone.

At first, it's easy to forget things and overlook simple details. For example, you won't forget bug spray or extra matches a second time. If rain is forecast, you'll erect your tent on low ground only once. Simple things like clearing debris from the tent site become instinctive.

You need some equipment. The most obvious item is a tent. Dome tents are popular, but the interior space is awkward. There's a multitude of 3-person dome tents selling for about $50. Most of them are about the right size for one medium-size adult and two small children. If you have doubts about size, see the tent erected before you purchase it.

A wall tent, with its rectangular floor, is popular and practical. A simple wall tent is usually a good buy. Common sizes are 8x10 or 9x12 feet. The smaller size is fine for four adults, the larger for six. To provide more privacy and to accommodate different sleeping habits, some families find two smaller tents are better than one large tent. Other families prefer one tent; they say it adds to the sharing and closeness of camping.

With a little care, tents last for years, be careful with sharp objects, keep sparks away, and never store a wet tent. If you must carry a wet tent home, dry it before packing it away.

Erect a tent in your backyard before your first campout. Bad weather, darkness, or confusing instructions can make it difficult to set up a new tent in a campground. The backyard trial also checks for missing parts.

Other major items you'll need are camping mattresses, sleeping bags or blankets, a food cooler, cooking stove, and lantern.

Air mattresses are popular, but some use foam pads and some prefer cots. Small children sleep well without special padding, a folded blanket work as a mattress for them.

Discount stores sell inexpensive summer-weight sleeping bags for about $15-20. These inexpensive bags are find for warm weather campouts, they're adequate down to about 50 degrees.

A food cooler costs between about $5 and $60 depending on size and construction. The cheaper ones are just insulating foam and are not very sturdy. Instead of using a large cooler for long campouts, we found it better to use two medium-sized coolers. Two medium-size coolers are easier to handle than a large one; we use one for weekend trips and use both for longer trips.

Cook either over a campfire or use a camping stove. Most campgrounds have firepits and some sell firewood, but cooking over a campfire in the rain isn't fun. Campfires may be prohibited if rainfall has been skimpy and there's a danger of forest fires. Most campers prefer a stove and acquire one eventually. Stoves using white gas are the most popular. Stoves using propane are a little safer and more convenient, but are more expensive to operate. Cook on a stove and use a campfire for fun things like popcorn, pudgy pies, marshmallows, and ghost stories. Try to have a campfire after sunset. It adds to the enjoyment.

You'll need a lantern for evening activities. White gas or propane lanterns provide the equivalent of a 100 watt bulb and they're fine for table games and overall illumination. These lanterns require mantles. Always carry extra mantles because they're very fragile. Battery lanterns are convenient, but they're dimmer and expensive to operate. A few campgrounds provide a 120-volt outlet for household electric lamps.

After dark, most children enjoy listening to stories or playing table games. Kids love to hear stories about their parents, all the funny or unusual things that happened during your youth.

Learning stars and constellations intrigue many families. Remember to let your children plan evening activities and then everyone participates, even if it means playing Old Maid. Remember the reason you're there - it's "A family campout."

Everyone has their own flashlight for safety. The batteries in children's flashlight never seem to last very long; carry extra batteries for them.

Expect to spend between $100 and $500 if you're buying everything for a first campout. Compare this amount with the cost of a two-day visit to an amusement park. Camping gear pays for itself the first time you use it and, then, the cost of camping is very low. Initially, renting is an inexpensive way to go if you're not quite sure if camping suits your family. It's usually possible to rent tents, cots, a stove, and a lantern locally.

Expect rain sooner or later on campouts, but don't let it bother you. A rainy day is a rare opportunity to share things with your family. Some campgrounds have a game pavilion for bad weather or bring your own tarpaulin for games on the picnic table. Consider spending the rainy day reading, hiking in the rain, or fishing. Have raincoats or ponchos with you.

Several consecutive days of rain does get tiresome. So, if the weather really gets bad, pack up and go home, don't be a hero. Learn from the experience and be able to cope better next time. Pushing your family into tolerating a bad situation will cause them to lose their love of camping and their interest in the outdoors, maybe forever. Eating is always a big part of camping. Picnic-type foods are fine, but don't hesitate to prepare any family favorite. Ovens, use on top of camping stoves, allow you to cook almost anything, even pizza.

Most campers use a camping box. It keeps everything together and could be as simple as a cardboard carton. Some use an old footlocker and some make their own from wood. Store dishes, games, and small items here. You'll always have these items with you if they're stored in your camping box.

Camping is for families, it's especially for families who want to stay close to nature and close to each other.

# WINTER CAMPING

In the fall, many campers throw their gear into the closet where it stays there until after Memorial Day. This limits their outdoor activity to less than one-half of the year.

You may be surprised to learn some people prefer off-season camping. There are distinct benefits: no crowds or noise, no bugs, spectacular scenery, and a wider selection of food because you have a natural refrigerator.

Activities will be a little different. You can still hike, but you may need snowshoes or skis and need more flashlights or a lantern for evenings.

Setting up a winter camp is a bit of an art form. Finding the right spot will partly determine how comfortable your night will be. Wind is an enemy. It rattles your tent, chills your hands as you cook or work, and generally makes life more difficult. An ideal site has a view, gets the first rays of the morning sun and is sheltered from the wind.

Don't set up in a valley. There can be 20 degrees difference in temperature between the top and bottom of a hill.

Once you've found a suitable spot, pack the snow by walking over it before you set up the tent. It's easier if you are wearing snowshoes or skis. Roll out your pads and sleeping bags inside the tent and you're home.

A winter tent needs to be larger than the tent you use during the summer, because you'll be spending more time inside and will need space to store your gear. A suitable tent will have a waterproof floor.

It's not ideal, but you can use a summer tent. If it requires tent stakes, you need to prepare deadmen. A deadman is a stick with a rope (that usually goes to a tent peg) tied to it. The stick with the rope is buried in the snow and the snow stepped on. A deadman holds much better than just a tent peg. A free-standing tent avoids the need for deadmen.

Ideally, a winter tent should have a vestibule for storing packs, wet outerwear and snowshoes, as well as used for cooking during stormy weather. Two doors and two vestibules are preferable, since they give you more storage space and ventilation.

A person exhales about a quart of water vapor overnight. If trapped inside the tent, that moisture will condense covering the walls and ceiling with frost. In the morning, that frost will melt and may dampen your sleeping bag. Down sleeping bags and clothing are useless when wet.

Winter tents have vents that can be left open in any weather. The vents are located near the top of the tent so moist air can escape.

After setting up camp, enjoy the winter scenery and look for animal tracks. The only thing you won't see is a lot of other people. When winter camping, you pretty much have the world to yourself.

You need more calories when camping in cold weather. Dinner often consists of a simple, calorie-rich stew.

Use a stove or a campfire for cooking. Firewood may be wet from the snow so a camper needs to be prepared with at least dry kindling. Some stoves will not function in cold weather. The best kind of stove for winter camping is one that uses white gas.

Melt snow to fill your water bottles, and boil another pot of water for hot cocoa or hot gelatin pudding (a sweet, caffeine-free alternative to coffee, tea or cocoa) as a before-bed drink.

After eating and cleaning up, it's time to sit around a campfire for a while. Then, remove boots and outer clothing and crawl into your sleeping bag.

Have a snack before retiring. Digesting food generates heat and keeps you warm. Keep a candy bar handy in case you wake up chilled.

Sleep with a hat, not only for warmth, but also to keep your sleeping bag clean. Wearing a hat prevent the oil from your hair from soiling the bag.

Put on dry socks to keep feet warm. To prevent feet from getting cold, wrap them in a jacket or extra insulating clothes or fill a container with hot water and place it at your feet.

Place wet boots in a plastic bag in the sleeping bag to keep them from freezing. Remove insoles and put them in your sleeping bag, but outside the waterproof bag. They will dry overnight. Stuff other items inside the sleeping bag: a full water bottle, camera and flashlight batteries.

It's best to use a mummy sleeping bag. It covers your neck and head. At least 25 percent of the heat emitted from the body is from the neck up. Covering neck and head also applies to daytime activities.

The warmth of a sleeping bag comes from the trapped air in the insulation. Estimate the temperature rating of a bag by measuring the loft, which is the thickness of both the top and bottom. With 4 inches of loft, a bag is good down to about 10 degrees; each additional inch is good for 10 more degrees.

Each inch of loft in a down sleeping bag provides a little more warmth than in a bag filled with synthetic fiber. But, a down bag is more expensive. If you need to buy another sleeping bag, choose a mummy bag with a temperature rating 10 degrees below the lowest night temperatures you expect. If you guess wrong on the lowest temperature, there are other ways to be comfortable.

Wear some clothes to bed and drape a blanket or poncho over the bag.

Whoever said that it's best to sleep naked inside a sleeping bag should do so on a winter night. Wear at least your long johns and dry socks.

It may be tempting to wear every bit of clothing to bed, but too much clothing can fill the sleeping bag, which compresses the insulation. This reduces the warmth of the bag. Pile clothes on top instead.

You may be surprised that water is important in winter camping. Cold, dry air dehydrates the body quickly and liquids are necessary to regulate metabolism. In cold weather camping, one of the best things you can do to stay healthy and warm is to drink water.

Even in freezing weather, look for flowing water. A lake may be frozen solid, but a stream or a tiny spring might be flowing. Filter or boil this water, freezing temperatures do not kill all the parasites in ground water. If unable to find flowing water, you'll have to melt snow.

If you expect to melt snow for drinking water, bring along black plastic trash bags. On a sunny day, shovel snow into them and set them in the sun. It takes an enormous amount of snow to make water, so as the snow starts to shrink in volume (which it will do as it starts to melt), add more snow to the bags.

In a couple of hours, you'll either have water, which can be funneled into a pot, or you'll have slush that will melt very quickly when it is heated.

For faster results, melt snow over either a campfire or a stove. Pour a little water into a pot before you add any snow. Once the water is warm, slowly add snow, wait until it warms up, then add more snow. Don't add it too quickly, or the melting process will slow down. Melting snow takes a lot of fuel and time, so try to find some running water.

Every time you go winter camping, have a Plan B just in case you encounter something you can't handle or there is a sudden change in the weather.

A possible problem is hypothermia. Shivering is often the first indication of this and it is the body's attempt to maintain its temperature. Shivering consumes a lot of energy, about the same as sawing wood. It delays hypothermia, but the heat loss must be stopped before the person's energy reserves are exhausted.

As a person's internal temperature – called the core temperature – drops further more symptoms appear. Improper behavior may occur in addition to sluggish speech and mental confusion. Victims lose the ability to use their hands and will have difficulty walking a straight line. These are indications of approaching hypothermia.

Hypothermia is easy to recognize in someone else. It's difficult to recognize in yourself because judgment and reasoning powers are rapidly impaired as the core temperature drops. Victims don't realize this is happening and quickly lose the ability to help themselves.

Here's how to cope with the early stages of hypothermia:

(1) Put on more clothing.

(2) Have something to eat when you first feel cold. Digestion generates internal heat.

(3) Exercise to increase internal heat production. However, vigorous physical activity will soon deplete a person's energy reserves. There's another problem with exercising. When a person's core temperature drops, blood flow to the extremities is restricted. Exercise will increase the core temperature and normal blood flow

will be restored to the hands and feet. This increases the heat loss, which is what caused the problem in the first place. Exercise is a temporary method to delay hypothermia until another solution is found.

(4) Get into a warm spot. It may be just a protected area with a campfire. Some "rough and ready" types may feel building a fire is admitting there's a problem. There is a problem and a fire could save that person's life.

Watch for frostbite. It causes white blotches, which appear first on hands, face and ears. Warm these areas as soon as possible.

Each camper needs a warm sleeping bag, a pad to put under it (to insulate from the cold ground), adequate personal clothing including wool socks, a warm hat and mittens. Plus perhaps a pair of snowshoes. There will not always be enough snow to use them. Snowshoes are useful when more than about 8 inches of snow is on the ground.

There's nothing wrong with a trial run in the backyard (it will amuse your neighbors) or near your car, so you can retreat if you have problem.

One problem of winter camping is how to spend up to 16 hours of darkness. A campfire is always welcome in the evening. In the tent, a headlamp helps when reading or playing a miniature board game.

Chances are that you'll find yourself ready for sleep long before your normal bedtime. Sleep comes quickly when in a warm sleeping bag after a good meal and a day of hiking in the cold.

If you have to answer a call of nature, just get up and do it instead of trying to cope with the discomfort. Enjoy the stars while you're outside. Guys can use a bottle to pee in and avoid the unpleasantness of stepping outside. Just close the container securely. Gals don't seem to have as much of a need to urinate at night.

In the morning, some campers lean out of their sleeping bag and heat water on a stove in the vestibule. In a few minutes, they enjoy hot cereal and coffee or cocoa. Breakfast in bed! How often do you get that at home? They then face a refreshing morning and another day of fun on skis or snowshoes.

You can be as comfortable in a winter camp as in summer. Perhaps more so, because the problem of winter -- cold – is sometimes easier to deal with than the problems of summer – the heat and bugs.

# THE SILENT KILLER

Have you ever shivered until your teeth chattered or found it difficult to talk properly in cold weather? Ever have problems walking because you were so cold? Perhaps you've gotten so cold you became extremely fatigued or even sleepy.

If your answer to any of these questions is yes, you were on the verge of becoming a victim of hypothermia. If the answer is no, you've been lucky - so far.

Hypothermia is the total physical and mental collapse that occurs when the vital organs of the body are chilled. A victim will often die without help. It is a concern when spending long periods outdoors during cold weather.

The weather doesn't have to be very cold to cause problems. Most hypothermia cases occur between 32 and 50 degrees F. Few outdoor enthusiasts realize these relatively mild temperatures can kill.

Body temperature starts to drop when the body heat is lost faster than it's replaced. The first warning sign is shivering. When the temperature of the vital organs, often called the core temperature, drops to 97 degrees shivering begins and becomes more violent if the core temperature continues to drop. Shivering consumes a lot of energy, about the same as sawing wood. It delays hypothermia, but you must do something immediately to reduce the heat loss from your body before energy reserves are depleted.

At a core temperature of 92 degrees, shivering stops and the muscles become rigid. A victim can act irrational and can't speak. Victims become lethargic. Now, they are usually incapable of helping themselves and need assistance to survive.

As the core temperature drops further, a person enters a stupor and loses consciousness. If the body temperature drops to this point, simple external warming won't correct the problem because the internal temperature will continue to drop even after external heat is applied. Professional medical help and equipment are required for the victim to survive. One method of emergency treatment is to have the victim breathe hot air, which quickly heats the heart and lungs.

At a core temperature of 78 degrees, death occurs.

Incapacitating, violent shivering can begin immediately after exposure and people have become victims of hypothermia in a matter of minutes.

Hypothermia often happens after clothing becomes wet. A serious threat occurs after falling into water. After climbing out, strip off your clothes and wring out as much water as possible before putting them on again. The insulating quality of most clothing is lost when wet and it greatly increases the loss of body heat. A person doesn't have to fall in water to get their clothing wet. Rain or perspiration does the same thing, but slower.

Hypothermia is easy to recognize in someone else. It's very difficult to recognize in yourself because mental capabilities are rapidly impaired. A cold body temperature strips you of judgment and reasoning power. A person doesn't realize this is happening. Victims quickly lose the mental and physical capability to help themselves. A person alone must be alert to this danger.

There are four ways to prevent hypothermia:
1) Get out of the cold into a warm shelter.
2) Reduce heat loss by wearing more clothing or other covering.
3) Exercise to increase heat production (a temporary solution).
4) Eat high-energy food (like a candy bar) to increase internal heat generation.

The nearest warm place for most people outdoors is often a sheltered spot with a fire, but a person in the early stages of hypothermia doesn't always consider this option. Building a fire seems like too much trouble with their impaired mental state. Some "rough and ready" types may feel that building a fire is admitting there's a problem. There is a problem and a fire is required. It could save that person's life.

The shelter must be out of the wind. Even a slight breeze lowers the effective ambient temperature and increases the probability of hypothermia.

The next best way to cope with hypothermia is extra clothing or other covering such as a blanket. When engaging in outdoor activity, have more clothing than you think you need -

particularly have a hat. About 25 percent of body heat is radiated from the neck up.

It's smart to carry a space blanket. It's a layer of aluminum foil supported on both sides by flexible plastic layers. The foil reflects body heat back and reduces heat loss. A space blanket costs only a few dollars and occupies little room in a pocket.

Exercise helps keeps you warm and prevents hypothermia. However, physical activity vigorous enough to keep you warm often will soon leave you exhausted and unable to continue with any exercise.

There's another problem with exercising. Physical activity really increases heat loss. When a person starts to become chilled, the body restricts blood flow to the extremities. After exercise, normal blood flow is restored to the hands and feet. This increases heat loss, which is what caused your problem in the first place. Exercise is a temporary way to delay hypothermia until you can find another solution.

Eating helps prevent hypothermia. Digestion generates internal heat and the food also provides energy. But eating cold food won't help if the core temperature has dropped to 94 degrees. At that point, the body starts to "shut down" and digestion stops.

When you are going to be out of doors for prolonged periods in cold weather, carry high-energy food with you and eat some at the first sign of a problem - when you start feeling cold. It's a good idea to bring along a hot beverage in an insulated container.

Items you should carry with you outdoors in cool weather include: a space blanket, candles or fire starters, matches, spoon, instant hot-beverage mixes, high energy foods, a whistle, and a plastic trash bag. Everything can be carried in a belt-pouch or pockets.

Cut a hole for your head in the trash bag to create an emergency garment or an instant wind break. Carry a Sierra cup (a small metal cup, with a wire handle, that also serves as a pot) or a tin can to heat water or food. A small metal box, such as a Band-Aid container, could carry most of the above items and also be used as a cooking pot. The candles or fire starters make it easier to build a fire. If you need help, the whistle can be heard over a greater distance than your voice and it's much easier than shouting.

Carry canned sardines. Granola bars, hard candy, nuts, powdered soups, an travel well in your pockets for either snacks or emergencies.

Being aware of the dangers of hypothermia is a good beginning for a safe excursion in cool weather. With a few items in your pocket and a little knowledge, you can spend an extended period of time outdoors in comfort and safety.

# MINIMIZE YOUR LOAD

Experts say backpackers are able to carry one-third of their body weight, but unless you're into pain, you'll enjoy backpacking more with a smaller load on your back. You really can reduce your pile of gear.

It takes a little thought and probably the purchase of some special equipment to lighten your load. With 20 pounds, all the normal needs and requirements for a safe, comfortable trip are included. It's easy to reduce your pack weight to less than 20 pounds. You may not want to reduce it so far because there are some shortcomings to this light load. You can go even lighter if you want; I've reduced my load to 10 pounds for a 3-day hike plus food and water. Some of you are going to say, "Oh, sure. This guy's full of baloney. Cutting weight to 10 pounds is impossible."

Read on.

At the end of a 14-mile hike, carrying one-third of my bodyweight, I was tired. My goal became a lighter load and I decided to try to avoid the mound of gear most backpackers feel is necessary. My effort has been to reduce weight and enjoy the outdoors more, not to become a survivalist or ignore safety and comfort.

I quickly discovered I needed to develop the proper attitude. I once met some teen-agers backpacking and saw a flashlight hanging on the outside of a pack, the kind that uses a 6-volt lantern battery. That flashlight weighed about 1-1/2 pounds. My backpacking flashlight weighs about 1.1 ounces with a spare bulb and battery. So, don't think flashlight, think "lightweight flashlight."

When you cultivate the proper attitude, begin weeding out unnecessary gear and replacing equipment with lightweight equivalents.

First, remove items from your pack if you never use them. The removal doesn't apply to emergency gear or a first-aid kit, of coursecourse of study

Evaluate each item in your pack, and use these thoughts to reduce their weight: Eliminate, combine, substitute, and modify. Here's a simple example of each. You might do some of these already.

Eliminate - Leave your kitchen knife and fork home. Most backpacking food can be eaten with a spoon (a plastic spoon, it's lighter).

Combine - Use a stuff bag for a pillow.

Substitute - carry a plastic cup instead of a metal one.

Modify - Repackage food and supplies. Take only what you'll need; eliminate the boxes and wrappings.

Got the idea? Don't try to reduce your load overnight. It takes thought and experiment to reduce weight and still meet your other needs. Here are some tips that work for me; they may not work for you.

Get rid of canteens - they're too heavy. Plastic jugs are fine.

Use tooth powder instead of toothpaste. It's easier to take just the required amount.

Wear T-shirts; they're lighter, because there's no collar and often no pockets.

Leave towels at home. Let everything air dry, or use a bandanna, a T-shirt, or a super-lightweight synthetic towel.

Consider leaving your heavy tent at home. Try a bivy for one person (one pound), instead of a tent (more than three pounds). Try a lightweight tarp, if insects and weather are not a problem.

In warmer weather, how about a military poncho-liner (one pound) instead of a sleeping bag (at least three pounds)? A poncho liner in a bivy keeps me warm down to about 55 degrees.

Don't carry an oil or candle lantern. A mini-flashlight is much lighter, smaller, more convenient, and brighter.

Can you eliminate a heavy stove and its fuel? Several wood-burning stoves, designed for backpacking, are available or you can make one from tin cans. It's not an open fire, and most backpacking areas allow them. Consider a Sterno or fuel-tablet stove for simple heating needs. Instead of a traditional 3-to-4 pound stove and fuel load, carry a wing stove that weighs three ounces (with six fuel tablets).

Eat only cold food, and eliminate your stove, fuel, pots, and pot-washing supplies. Cold food for all meals doesn't suit everyone, so try it at home before a hike.

Eliminate your water filter. Treat water with chemicals instead. Saves a pound or more.

Replace a soap dish with a plastic bag. Of course, carry a sliver, not the whole bar of soap; if you carry liquid soap, use a small container.

Wash clothes instead of trying to carry enough clean ones. Wash them in a basin made from your poncho, groundcloth, or a plastic bag.

Don't carry a separate groundcloth; use your poncho. Carry several plastic bags instead of a poncho. In case of rain, tie a bag over your pack; cut holes in another for you head and arms. Then use the bags as a groundcloth at night. This saves about two pounds.

Get a smaller pack. It encourages finding ways to reduce weight and bulk (a smaller pack is also a lighter pack).

Don't carry a full container of anything. Repack seasonings, bug repellent, and first-aid supplies in smaller containers. Sandwich or Ziploc bags are great for most items. Some bug repellents destroys plastic, so test first.

Don't carry a full roll of toilet paper.

Many people automatically pack their wallets. Carry only a few items instead, perhaps a credit card, driver's license, fishing permit, and a few dollars in a waterproof plastic bag. Include coins for an emergency phone call. I eliminated my wallet and reduced my load by six ounces.

Don't worry about clean clothes for the trip home. Leave a fresh set in your car.

Do you carry binoculars for nature study or bird watching? Use a monocular instead. Also, consider a mini-tripod to replace a full-sized one, or make a tripod by lashing three sticks together, spread the legs, and then set your camera on top. Some hikers use a monopod as a walking stick.

Some packers go to unusual lengths to reduce weight. My son cut his toothbrush handle in half and then drilled holes in the

43

rest of it. A friend carries only a light windbreaker in the summer. He uses his poncho or sleeping bag for additional warmth. Another friend doesn't carry a sleeping bag; He wears warm clothes for sleepwear, and, of course, the clothes are available during the day.

Some hikers think a large hiking group reduces everyone's load; it does, but only a little. Sharing the weight works with just the community gear, such as a tent, stove, lantern, water filter, and first-aid kit. With two people, each load is reduced by perhaps four pounds.

These tips lighten your load, but other ideas also increase comfort while hiking.

Most backpackers know how to load a pack, but a few don't. A novice, incorrectly, tends to put heavy items at the bottom of the pack. Load heavy items high in the pack and close to you. Why? People lean until their center of gravity is over their ankles. A pregnant woman leans backward, and backpackers lean forward. Leaning puts unnecessary strain on muscles and causes fatigue. Leaning is minimized with the load high and close to you. An internal-frame pack holds the load closer to your body than an external-frame pack.

Do you use a walking stick? Among other things, using one allows arms and shoulders to assist weary legs.

The way you walk is a factor. Point your toes straight-ahead (instead of splayfooted), and walk as if your legs were connected to your stomach instead of your hips. Both techniques increase stride length. Lengthen it by only one inch, and you'll travel about nine feet farther every minute. You cover more distance without additional effort.

Rest often; every 45 minutes works fine for most of us. Stop and rest before you become tired; you'll be able to hike further and feel better. A rest break should be 10 to 15 minutes, because muscles stiffen with longer breaks, and 15 minutes is an efficient rest period. About 1/3 of the lactic acid in your muscles dissipates in the first 15 minutes of a rest period; another 15 minutes removes only five percent more.

If you must climb a steep hill, do it easier by taking short steps instead of a normal stride. Short steps are like lifting one pound 100 times vs. lifting 100 pounds once. It helps to lean forward more while walking uphill. Small steps are easier going downhill also.

The ultimate in load reduction is to carry nothing. I met an older man with all his gear tied to a luggage cart. He said, "My back is the problem. Either I use a cart, or give up backpacking."

He installed a longer handle with a shoulder strap to allow easier pulling. It looked a little awkward, but he claimed it worked fine. He admitted to carrying the cart over some rough spots.

Eliminate some weight by caching supplies and water on the trail at spots accessible by car. Spot water in plastic milk jugs (carry out the empty jugs). Cache food also, but protect it from scavengers: Either hang food from trees, or put it in an adequate container on the ground.

The rope and plastic bags used to hang cached supplies are easy to pack out. You may need to return to the cache location by car to retrieve the ground storage container.

Remember my ten-pound pack? Here's what I carry on some warm-weather trips:

Day pack, 14 ounces; fanny pack, 4 ounces; wing stove, 3 ounces; bivy, 16 ounces; poncho liner, 16 ounces; water jug, 3 ounces; cooking pot-cup, 6 ounces; mini-flashlight, 1 ounce; poncho, 16 ounces.

Trash bags, 2 ounces; toilet paper/trowel, 4 ounces; extra clothes, 42 ounces; compass and map, 2 ounces; rope, 4 ounces; sleeping pad, 12 ounces; first-aid kit, 4 ounces; miscellaneous (soap, knife, water-purifier tablets, matches), 7 ounces.
Total weight is 9 pounds, 12 ounces. Slightly less than the 10 pounds promised. With this limited gear, some restrictions are automatic: It can't be too cold, and no photography or fishing.

I carry some this in a fanny pack because my daypack isn't quite big enough to handle everything. I also use the fanny pack for day hiking from a base camp.

If I carry only cold food, another half-pound is eliminated. Add about two pounds a day for food, plus four pounds for two quarts of water, and I start a 3-day hike with less than 20 pounds. You can almost jog with a 20-pound load. I finish with only ten pounds.

Develop the correct attitude and you'll generate your own weight-saving ideas. Reduce your load - hike farther and enjoy backpacking more.

clothes, 42 ounces; compass and map, 2 ounces; rope, 4 ounces; sleeping pad, 12 ounces; first-aid kit, 4 ounces; miscellaneous (soap, knife, water-purifier tablets, matches), 7 ounces.

Total weight is 9 pounds, 12 ounces. Slightly less than the 10 pounds promised. With this limited gear, some restrictions are automatic: It can't be too cold, and no photography or fishing.

Develop the correct attitude and you'll generate your own weight-saving ideas. Reduce your load - hike farther and enjoy backpacking more.

# BACKPACKING WITH KIDS

Your kids are growing up, and maybe you're thinking it's time for them to join you on your hiking and backpacking adventures. There are good reasons to take your children. As backpackers, children learn to enjoy the outdoors and to be self-sufficient. There also is a subtle and different parent-child bonding that takes place while backpacking.

Family backpacking can be a wonderful experience, but you can ruin it for everyone by pushing too hard. Here are some guidelines for backpacking with children.

Don't rush out to plan a long hike. Start much slower. Hike at least one short weekend trip before making other plans. Some children aren't ready for it. Others will never like it. You had better be aware of either situation before dragging them along on a lengthy backpack.

Judge a child's capacity during short walks around the neighborhood. If a child is able to walk three miles without resting, then he or she should be capable of covering the same distance on an easy trail, with rest breaks, and a reasonably loaded pack.

Infants, old enough to hold their heads erect, adjust well to a baby pack. They seem to find the gentle motion soothing, and often fall asleep, but protect them from sunburn. When awake, infants enjoy looking around or playing with your ears.

There are other considerations with infants. You must carry the child plus a heavy load of special food, diapers, and extra clothing. Diapers are the biggest concern; they're bulky and troublesome. Disposable diapers decompose very slowly, so pack them out. Soiled diapers are lighter if you hang them (away from camp) to dry. Some feel that washing cloth diapers reduces the load. It does, but washing diapers on the trail isn't very sanitary for the baby or the environment.

As long as your infant is still in diapers, you may want to restrict your activities to day-hikes.

Kids between two and four years old can be tough hikers, but they need frequent breaks. Stop every 15 minutes to rest or sightsee, and walk slow because their legs are a lot shorter than yours. Don't expect them to carry anything, but if they want to help, give them a small pack with lunch, snack food, or a canteen; then their load lightens quickly. Some two-to-four-year old children will surprise you with their hiking ability, but don't expect more than about three miles a day.

Children five-to-seven-years old are less demanding on their adult companions, but at this age they are still unable to carry all their own gear. Try giving them a day pack loaded with just their own clothing. Plan to hike up to four miles a day. This age group has limited endurance and a short attention span.

Older children, ages eight-to-ten, can hike up to about six miles a day on easy trails. Work up to this distance. Let them carry their own clothes and their sleeping bags. Give them a trail map, and allow them to track your progress. Stop to rest often.

From 11 to 13, an adolescent with a little conditioning can hike up to about nine miles a day. Again work up to this level. Adolescents should be able to carry all of their own gear, plus a little extra.

With sufficient rest stops, conditioned teen-agers can cover the same distances as adults and with nearly the same loads. However, during their rapid growth spurts, teen-agers lose some endurance and may be unable to hike as far or carry as much as they did a year ago. Be aware of this and allow for longer rest breaks if you see unexpected fatigue.

Hikes with children should be planned to allow for free time at the end of the day. Kids may want to fish, swim, play games, toss a Frisbee, or just sit and read.

Don't push past these guidelines unless you know your children can handle it. If you push pass their limits, they will not want to hike next time.

Experts argue about the proper load for backpackers. Most agree that you should not carry more than one-third of your body weight. Even so, this is too much for pleasant hiking. Don't turn yourself into a pack mule. Carry less than 25 percent of your body weight and try to reduce it even more. As you hike, watch your kids; if you see fatigue, offer to carry some of their load. Don't force a heavy load on your youngster.

It should be a family effort from the beginning. Let everyone share in the plans. Allow your children to select some of the food and let everyone take a turn preparing the food or cleaning up after meals. One of my sons is a fabulous cook. I suspect the seeds were planted on our early backpacking trips.

Let children pack their own gear, but inspect it; kids have unusual ideas about what is essential. On his first backpacking trip, one of my youngsters filled his pack with books and managed to find room for only one extra pair of socks. Another son wanted to pack a huge mound of clothes and then thoughtfully tossed in two boxes of Band-Aids.

Allow a small child to bring a favorite toy, perhaps a stuffed animal, a doll, or a toy car. We also bring lightweight family games for evening activities and assign the game selection to a child. Don't let your child pack a game with many small pieces, like Monopoly®. One of my kids selected a game in which individual scores are tabulated on paper. Of course, we could share one pen among the four players. Instead, my 8-year-old son asked, "What color pen do you want?" In his pack, he had 16 ballpoint pens. Each of us had a choice of four different colors to keep our score.

Some backpacking gear is available in small sizes. That's fine, but high-quality gear for children usually is a waste of money; kids grow too fast. Consider modifying adult backpacking equipment. One youngster was too small for an adult-sized pack, but could carry a heavier load than would fit in a day pack. We moved the hip belt of an adult pack so the belt went around the outside of the pack frame. It worked fine. We were careful not to overload him. Another family in the same situation loaded a day pack with heavier items rather than try to use a larger pack. In both cases, the child volunteered to carry a heavier load.

Allow children to carry food and other supplies. As these items are consumed, their packs become lighter. Adults should carry the permanent gear, such as the stove and tent.

Be sure to pack warm garments for children. They have lower tolerance for cold temperatures. Include an extra set of dry clothing - kids like to get wet.

Young children tend to wander off, so constant awareness is required. Warn children not to roam, and then tell them to sit and wait if they find themselves lost. Hang a whistle around their neck and tell them to blow it every few minutes. Fortunately, children usually do the correct thing when they're lost; they stop and sit.

Point out animal tracks, wildflowers, and bird nests. Help children to identify birds, trees, and stars. You might not know enough to teach your children, but then you can learn together. A backpack trip can be a marvelous educational experience for the entire family.

# SOLO BACKPACKING

You've been a backpacker for a while and it's harder and harder to find hiking companions. Or your children are grown and have other priorities in their busy lives.

Maybe you do find other hikers, but it's difficult to find a compatible time or a trail that fits everyone. Or you need some space and want to get away by yourself for a time. The thing to do is backpack alone - solo backpacking.

Maybe your first thought is "No way!" But don't be hasty. Solo backpacking allows you to hike when and where it suits you because you sacrifice some of your freedom hiking with others. Hike alone and companions can't slow you down or hurry you.

If you're up tight and need to get away from everything, hike solo. Some people never experience solitude and here's one way to spend time alone. Solo backpacking allows you to find yourself or lose yourself. Learn to enjoy the tranquility of the trail. Solo hikers acquire a greater kinship with nature.

Some people are concerned with the dangers while hiking alone, they are afraid. Certainly safety must be considered, but you are probably safer walking on a trail than you are walking at night on most city streets. Sometimes the real reason is people are not comfortable alone. They're not totally comfortable being alone anytime or anywhere. You must be comfortable by yourself to be a solo hiker.

People usually enjoy solo backpacking after climbing over the first hurdles. Backpacking is intended to enhance a wilderness experience and that means hiking alone is preferable to traveling with a group for a true wilderness experience.

There are disadvantages; there's no one to help if you have trouble. You must be able to handle everything you encounter. You can't rely on someone else bringing the matches or the can opener you forgot. If something breaks, you must have the means to fix it or be able to do without. Your load will be a little heavier with the equipment normally shared with companions. You must carry shelter, stove, and pots. You should also carry a water filter, first aid kit, repair kit, and a flashlight.

You might think at first these items will add a ton to your pack. With a group, you share a shelter with another hiker; you might carry the tent and the water filter; your companion carries the stove, pots, first aid kit, and lantern. So, you carry about half of these items now even with a companion.

These items, carried solo, add only about five or six pounds to your load. You should be able to handle this and there are ways to reduce even this increased weight. For example, you now share a heavier tent with companions. Instead, use a light one-man tent or a bivy to reduce the weight. You need fewer and smaller pots and dishes. You don't need a lantern for the campsite, a small flashlight will do for a solo hiker.

With a little pre-planning, you may be able to spot water and food at a trail-road crossing to reduce the pack weight further. Perhaps you can use a campfire and eliminate the weight of a stove. Going solo, you could wind up with a lighter pack by planning everything better.

To minimize any danger, leave your itinerary with a responsible person containing instructions to contact authorities if you do not return before a prearranged date and time. Define your route, expected campsites, and the estimated time of arrival at road crossings along the trail. Not the exact time of arrival, a notation on the map of "I'll be there late Friday morning" is OK.

This information is also invaluable if you're needed to return home for a family emergency. With an itinerary provided by a friend or relative, police and park rangers can locate you easier. Plan ahead enough to define your route and allow some slack in your schedule. You don't want to rush your wilderness experience.

Leave the phone number of the park office or the nearest police station with your itinerary. Don't forget to include any side trips you might try. Stop at the park office to tell them about your hike. The park rangers will be able to offer advice about treacherous portions of the trail, recent incidents of vandalism, or campsites to avoid.

Don't leave your agenda displayed on the dashboard of your car. Leaving those long-range plans visible is an invitation to thieves. If you are concerned about leaving your car alone for several days, consider public transportation or have a friend drive you to and from the trailheads.

Of course, these arrangements won't help much if you trip and break a leg on a lonely portion of trail on the first day of a week-long hike. So be careful, be wary of treacherous areas and don't do dumb things like hiking at night.

If you are injured and can't travel, use your signaling devices. A whistle and flares are lightweight and attract nearby people. A mirror, used properly, and a smoky fire attract searching aircraft.

Be prepared. Carry maps and a compass. Know how to use them. Use a checklist as you pack your gear to ensure nothing is forgotten. Carry survival gear.

Being alone, some discretion is required. Don't camp near roads where you might encounter troublemakers. If you meet other hikers on the trail, trust your instincts. If you have a bad feeling, mention that your group is right behind you and don't mention your future campsites or your route.

If the weather turns sour or your feet become sore, don't be a hero. Cut your hike short. Every third or fourth day, plan for a short hike. Wash clothes, relax, or fish on these easy days.

Don't plan a lengthy hike for your first solo; try a weekend or an overnight first. Pack a book or a lightweight radio if the need for companionship arises. Use a journal to record your thoughts. Hiking alone allows you to spend more time investigating plants or birds if these interest you. Allow time for this in your itinerary.

Stop early to avoid a "I must stop here" situation and also to allow time for all the chores. You must build a fire, get water, cook, and set up camp.

You might be more comfortable hiking on familiar trails, those you've hiked previously with others. Other solo hikers prefer to hike new trails because you are not tempted to repeat the route or stay at the campsites used on previous group trips and everything will be fresh.

One minor problem mentioned by solo hikers. Returning to civilization is marked by an increased awareness of noise, traffic jams, and crowds of people. The disadvantages of civilization are more apparent after a wilderness experience.

A solo backpack is a wonderful unique experience. If you are a nature lover, you must try backpacking alone.

# DRY YOUR HIKING FOOD

Would you like fresh fruit and vegetables on a long backpack? In addition to being healthy, fresh produce supplements that pasta dish and adds zest to your meals. However, fresh produce often spoils quickly and maybe you've noticed it's heavy and bulky.

So we tend to omit tasty and nutritious produce on our backpacking menus. Your health and taste buds suffer without fresh fruit and vegetables. However, there's a way to have them on long hikes without adding much weight.

It's simple -- dehydrate your food. Drying has been used since ancient times to preserve food and it's still one of the best methods. You can dehydrate almost everything produce, meats, and soups. Dry sauces for pasta or rice to eliminate the weight of containers. Include dried food on your menus to benefit your health, wallet, and eating pleasure. And best of all, dried food lightens your load.

It's not difficult; you can start by using your kitchen oven. Set your oven to its lowest temperature, place the food inside, leave the oven door ajar, and wait. Simple? Sure, but with a few more details, you'll achieve better results.

The open oven heats your house, so it's best to dry food on cool days. The oven temperature should be below 130 degrees and this may be difficult with some ovens. A higher temperature both destroys vitamins and hardens the outside of the produce that prevents the interior from drying thoroughly. The moist interior causes spoilage later. Ideal drying temperature for most foods is about 115 degrees. Herbs and spices are dried best at about 100 degrees.

If using energy to heat the oven bothers you and if the weather cooperates, use your car as a dehydrator. Park your car in the sun with the food on trays inside. Open the windows about an inch and hope the food dries completely before sunset. If it doesn't dry thoroughly, store the partly dried produce in your refrigerator overnight and try again the next day.

An oven or car works but they have insufficient temperature control. After experiencing the benefits of dried food, improve your results by purchasing, or making, a dehydrator. Several commercial units are available starting at about $30. Units with both a thermostatic control (to maintain proper temperature) and a fan (to evenly distribute the air) are best.

Start by drying fruit instead of vegetables; try apples, pears, pineapples, bananas, apricots, or watermelon first. Dried fruit is often tastier than fresh because the flavor is concentrated. Children and adults love dried watermelon and don't be surprised if everyone prefers it over candy. Dried fruit retains all nutrients (except vitamin C). We tend to eat more fruit when it's dried, so we consume more of their minerals, vitamins, antioxidants, and fiber.

Fruit should be washed, peeled and then sliced to the roughly the same thickness. For apples, a corer is convenient, but you can slice them with a knife. It's faster to cut apples into wedges, but don't cut them too thick. To keep drying times reasonably short, maximum thickness should be about 3/8 inch. The same technique is used for most other fruits.

Dried fruit is flexible and bends easily. With a little experience, it's easy to tell when it's dry enough (it takes 4 to 24 hours). It's better to over-dry a little than under-dry.

Just toss most dried fruits into a storage container, but some fruits, including pineapples and watermelons, dry sticky. Dusting the pieces with flour or corn starch before storage helps to avoid a wad of these fruits later. Another way is to use plastic-wrap or waxed paper between layers of the sticky dried fruit.

Dry applesauce by spreading it evenly on sheets of plastic-wrap on the trays in your dehydrator. When it's dry enough, separate the partly dried sauce from the plastic-wrap, and continue the drying. For storage, roll while it's still warm. Use this method to dry sauces for pasta.

Make fruit leathers the same way as applesauce. Process fruit in a blender until it's a puree and then spread it on plastic-wrap. Combine different fruits in your blender for a wonderful variety of flavors. Apples mix well with most other fruits. For tasty leathers, add spices to the mixture for an infinite number of taste treats. Try cinnamon, vanilla, allspice, brown sugar, ginger, or nutmeg. Mix in a little honey if the fruit is tart; add about a teaspoon of honey to two cups of puree.

The drying process discolors some fruits. It's not really the drying; it's the exposure to air. The taste is not affected, but you may want to minimize the color change. Reduce the discoloration by soaking the fruit for a minute before drying in a mixture of a pint of water and either a teaspoon of lemon juice or six vitamin C tablets.

Eat dried fruit as is or soak in water first. The reconstituted fruit tastes almost the same as fresh. Mix reconstituted fruit in gelatin desserts and yogurt or use small pieces in cakes and cookies.

It's more involved to dry vegetables because blanching is usually recommended. Blanching stops the slow enzyme action which toughens vegetables and spoils their flavor. Blanching also breaks down the internal cell walls allowing thorough drying.

After peeling and slicing the vegetables, blanch them by plunging into boiling water or exposing to steam. Steam blanching is preferred because it removes less of the beneficial water-soluble vitamins and minerals.

Blanch vegetables until they appear translucent. Blanching time varies with vegetable hardness. In steam, hard vegetables (corn, carrots, potatoes, etc.) need about four minutes; soft vegetables (such as celery, greens, or asparagus) -- half as long. Blanching in boiling water needs about one-third less time. There's no need to blanch onions, mushrooms, garlic, cucumbers, tomatoes, or peppers.

Vegetable drying times are a little longer than for fruit. Vegetables dry hard and brittle. They must be reconstituted before using. There are several ways to reconstitute foods:
1) Soak in cold water for between one and five hours. Reconstitute vegetables for your evening meal while you hike.
2) Soak in hot water for about 20 minutes.
3) Steam in the same utensil you used to blanch them. This is the fastest way and takes about ten minutes or so.
4) Add dried vegetables directly to soups or stews and allow them to reconstitute while cooking, but they will be softer if presoaked in water for an hour first.

When reconstituting foods, vegetables take longer than fruits and smaller pieces reconstitute faster (shredded or grated are fastest). Smaller pieces also dry faster.

Reconstituted vegetables are seldom consumed by themselves; they are usually mixed into stews and soups. Try them also as toppings for pizza, in omelets, or in dips.

Most backpackers prefer zippered plastic bags for storage. Then each bag contains the dried food for one meal. You can use glass or plastic containers and portion it out later if that suits you. Dried fruit and vegetables can be kept for years; however they do deteriorate slowly. They're still edible, but the taste suffers somewhat. Store dried food in a freezer or refrigerator to prolong storage life, but your dried food will probably be eaten before shelf life becomes a problem.

Additional information about food drying is available. A skimpy booklet with the basics of food drying is often included with purchased dehydrators. One of the best guidebooks is How to Dry Foods by Deanna DeLong. It covers optimum drying techniques for specific produce and has many great recipes.

Experiment to discover your own favorites. Dried food saves money, is healthy and it's lightweight. Enjoy.

# PREDICTING WEATHER THE NATURAL WAY

Complain about the weather. Go ahead – all of us do it. Often, though, you need to know what the weather is going to be like, especially when planning a hunting or fishing trip. You can rely on newspaper forecasts, but they are often obsolete by the time they are published, or do not apply to the area in question. Or you can watch television, where you'll hear where the hottest and coldest spots in the United States are that day and what year the local temperature records were set. The forecaster will then show how the high- and low-pressure areas will move over the next few days. But do you really want this information?

Then the forecaster might say, "I think we'll have about a 50 percent chance of light rain tomorrow, but it's a little too soon to tell for sure." Or maybe you'll hear, "it's going to be partly clear." Does this mean anything to you? Did the forecast help you plan your trip?

Forecasters use computers and a multitude of data to predict weather. They claim their forecasts are about 80 percent accurate. This is a little misleading. Fait-weather predictions are easy to forecast, and these are part of the claimed 80 percent accuracy. During good-weather cycles, most of us can guess and be right 80 percent of the time. Where most forecasts fail is during bad weather, and this is when you really need better predictions. Unexpected weather could change your trip into a miserable experience or even a life-threatening one.

So, what can you do? Try forecasting the weather yourself. Perhaps you can do as well, or better, that the weather bureau or that "50 percent of light rain" personality.

You probably know a few simple forecasting tips already. You might realize that a red sunset means good weather and a red sunrise usually forecast rain. It's remembered easily with a rhyme: Red sky at night, sailors' delight/Red sky at morning, sailors take warning.

Low-angle sunlight refracts in the dusty, dry air of a high-pressure area. If the redness occurs at sunset, the dry air is west of us and is approaching in the normal flow of weather patterns in the Northern Hemisphere. If the redness occurs at sunrise, the dry air is east of us, and this increases chances that the next air mass will be wet. Still, a red sky at night is a better indicator of good weather than a red sunrise is an indicator of bad weather.

Other rhymes may also be familiar: Ring around the moon, rain before noon/Ring around the sun, rain before night is done. Rings around the moon or sun are caused by cirrus clouds. Cirrus clouds appear hundreds of miles ahead of warm fronts and their associated rain. So cirrus clouds indicate no rain for a while, but it's coming, probably in 12 to 18 hours. The bigger the ring, the thicker the cloud layer and the nearer the rain.

Here's another: Grass is dry before morning/Look for rain before night. Clear night skies allow the temperature to drop low enough for moisture in the air to condense as dew. No clouds mean no approaching warm front, and no rain. If the temperature rises during the night, it means increasing cloud cover and approaching rain. Sometimes fog occurs in the morning. Fog indicates the temperature has dropped due to clear skies and that there is no wind. High-pressure areas are characterized by clear skies and low winds.

Sound and smell are also tools to predict weather. If sounds seem louder or travel farther, rain is coming. Why? Humid air, associated with incoming low-pressure areas, transfers sound better than the dry air of high-pressure areas.

If odors are stronger, it also indicates rain on the way. Plants release more aromatic oils in the high humidity of approaching bad weather. Other odors are also more pronounced as bad weather approaches. Scents are weaker in high-pressure areas because they are squeezed tight to the source. In low pressure, odors are released more easily, and so we notice them more. We sometimes subconsciously observe this and say, "It smells like rain." We also emit more body odor as a storm heads our way. Increased odor near urban sewers also indicate approaching bad weather.

Wind is another weather indicator. If it's from the east or south, expect rain. Wind from the northeast may bring two or three days of rain starting in 24 hours. Westerly winds bring fair weather. Fair winds usually come from the southwest in the summer and the northwest in the winter.

Winds are calm ahead of a wide warm front, so if then rain appears before the wind, expect a long rain. If the wind arrives first, it's a narrow cold front and the storm will soon end. Calm winds usually mean warmer temperatures. Expect cooler weather with increasing winds.

If temperatures increase during a rainstorm, expect more and heavier precipitation soon. It's because a warm front is passing and the rains extends on both sides on a warm front.

When you see the underside of tree leaves, rain is coming. Why? Leaves grow normally with the prevailing fair-weather winds. Winds from any other than the fair-weather direction blow the leaves differently and they tend to flip over. Thus, the under sides of leaves appear when the wind shifts from it's usual fair-weather direction.

If the wind is shifting in a counterclockwise direction (for example, shifting from west to southwest), expect poorer weather within 24 hours. If the shift is clockwise (for example, from south to southwest), expect the weather to improve.

Tracking low-pressure areas provides a clue as to how the bad weather is moving. Turn your back to the wind and extend your left arm out to the side. Your arm points roughly toward the low-pressure area. It's actually a little behind you, but straight out to the side is close enough. Assume the weather system is moving east. With several observations, you may be able to determine if the storm is passing north or south, or heading directly toward you.

Animals and insects are helpful in predicting weather. For example, when ants walk in a straight line, rain is coming, and when they walk in circles, or randomly, it means good weather. Birds, insects, and most small animals are noisy were bad weather is 24 hours away and become quieter as bad weather approaches. Flies are the exception. They become more troublesome as a storm approaches. If birds are taking dirt baths, it will probably rain within 12 hours.

Birds fluffing their feathers, feeding ravenously, or gathering in groups are other signs of bad weather. If birds feed in then rain, expect the rain to continue for a while. In a short storm, the birds would wait to feed. A lot of bird activity occurs right before a storm. Spider webs absorb moisture and break more easily in the high humidity associated with an approaching low-pressure area. If you see a spioder spinning a web, it's probably not going to rain for a while.

Birds fly high, clear blue sky/Birds fly low, rain we shall know. One theory as to why this happens is that air pressure drops as a low-pressure area approaches. It's harder for birds to fly in the thinner air, so their flights are lower and shorter than normal.

Robins build fragile nests. They roost to hold the nest together in approaching storms. If you see a robin hopping around during breeding season, expect fair weather. In some areas, deer tend to move downhill a day or two before a storm hits. If deer feed in the early afternoon, expect bad weather within 24 hours.

Twinkling stars indicate strong upper-altitude winds, which are usually a warning that bad weather will arrive in two or three days. If stars appear bluer than normal, it's also a sign that rain is coming. Humid air absorbs the red coloring from the starlight, causing them to appear to be a slightly different color.

Check your campfire smoke. If it rises quickly, you can expect clear weather. If the smoke drifts, then settles lower, expect rain. The same is true of chimney smoke. In a high-pressure area, the temperature decrease rapidly with height and allows the slowly cooling smoke to continue rising. In a low-pressure area, the temperature changes less with altitude. Smoke quickly becomes the same temperature as the air, and stops rising.

People tend to feel worse in general as humidity increases and bad weather approaches. If you experience more headaches, sleeplessness, or arthritis pain, bad weather could be approaching. Children and pets often misbehave more as a storm nears.

If there are clouds that look like fish scales (called a "mackerel" sky), expect a lasting rain in eight to 24 hours. These clouds appear in advance of warm fronts. Note that a mackerel sky indicates that it will not rain for at least eight hours, but rain is coming. You can't accurately predict the weather more than two or three days ahead, but it helps to know that weather patterns tend to repeat on a five-to-seven-day cycle. This is why it sometimes seems to rain every weekend. Try using these tips to predict the weather. Some clues work better than others, or are easier to observe in your particular area. Don't rely on only one clue, it could be a freak event. But when several weather signs say the same thing, believe them. Any fewer than three clues and your prediction should be "50 percent chance of light rain, but it's a little too early to tell for sure.

# Finding Your Way

Ever been lost? It's not a pleasant experience, but why should any hunter worry about this. No one becomes lost while hunting. Most of the time you're sitting still anyway. Never follow a wounded animal and you can't get lost. Never stray off the trail or go on a side trip and you'll be fine. But, think for a second. The only people who become lost are the ones who never expect it and never prepare for the possibility. What happens if you lose your way? Are you prepared for the unexpected?

Being lost may be a frightening experience or a piece of cake. It may mean your death or just a minor inconvenience. Your first reaction makes a big difference on the outcome.

At the first sign of a problem, stop and think. Some say hug a tree. Sounds silly, but you're not going to meander aimlessly with your arms wrapped around a tree. Reconstruct your recent movements and remember where you last knew your location. Remember the direction traveled since then and the direction of the sun and wind while walking.

Perhaps you'll quickly realize you just walked down that hill over there or the sun was in your face as you moved. Mentally retracing your steps may quickly solve your confusion.

If pausing to think doesn't help, what then? Look at your map and compass. What? No map or compass? Your problem is becoming serious.

A map and compass are invaluable when you're lost, but don't think they alone will save you. If you're unable to locate your departure and destination on the map or you don't know what direction you've been traveling since you started, a map and compass are not effective tools.

A compass helps on a return trip only if you used it on the way out. Knowing which way is north isn't going to lead back to camp or the trail if you don't know where they are. Use a compass to help monitor direction as you hike. Continually observe your heading to avoid walking in circles.

Everyone tends to walk in circles. People are unsymmetrical, one leg is longer or stronger than the other which affects the way we walk. Almost everyone veers off to one side and some hikers complete a circle in 30 minutes.

Other factors affect our path. Most people tend to move around an obstruction by moving to the right and this changes direction a tiny bit at each obstacle. People tend to turn away from a high wind or the bright sun. On sloping terrain everyone tends to walk downhill.

Knowing this helps keep a straight path but the best way is pick a prominent terrain feature in the proper direction, go to it, and then pick another landmark using some directional indicator such as compass.

Several types of compasses are available, some pin onto clothing, some use a lanyard, and some mount in knife handles.

With a pin-on compass it's easy to monitor your travel -just glance at it occasionally. Reaching into a pocket for a compass is tiresome. Pick one that suits you, but purchase a liquid-filled compass. A liquid-filled model is easier to read because it stabilizes faster.

A compass points to magnetic north, not true north. The difference between the two is called variation. The agonic line, or line of zero variation, runs approximately through Milwaukee, Chicago, Indianapolis, Knoxville, and Savannah. Elsewhere a compass points east or west of true north. Variation in the Northeast is about 24 degrees west and is about 20 degrees east in the Northwest part of the Continental United States.

West variation means a compass points west of true north. Add west variation to your desired direction and subtract east variation. For example, if you want to travel due east (90 degrees); and the variation is 10 degrees west, add 90 plus 10 for a compass heading of 100 degrees. Hiking a compass indication of 100 degrees is moving directly east. Use the memory trick, "East is least, west is best" to determine if you add or subtract variation.

Topographic maps indicate the local variation. If the local variation is less than 5 degrees or so, it's not worthwhile worrying about for most hikers.

A topographic map allows preplanning your route and becoming familiar with the terrain. Will you follow a ridge? Cross a stream? Walk uphill? Make a mental note as you encounter these terrain features while hiking.

Carry a map and compass, preplan your route, hug a tree if confused and you should not have a problem.

OK, instead you really blew it. Perhaps you wandered off the trail to see something and didn't pay attention to anything else. Now, you have no idea where you are, maybe only a vague idea where the trail is, no map or compass, and no idea of direction.

I heard a story. A man at a remote fishing camp in Canada wandered away from the cabin. He became disoriented at dusk and frantically raced around searching for the cabin. After an hour of panic, he realized he had a real problem. He had traveled several miles and didn't have a clue how to find the cabin. Why did he panic? He said later that he felt silly about losing his way and didn't want his fishing companions to laugh at him.

He finally sat down and thought about his predicament. The only thing he remembered about the terrain was a railroad about 100 miles east of the cabin that lead eventually to a town. He felt the chance of being found quickly by a search party was slim. He decided to reach the railroad track and follow it to the settlement. Without survival equipment, he knew it would be rough.

It took 100 days to walk to the town. When he first became confused, he wasn't more than a few hundred yards from camp. If he waited for daylight, instead of those 100 tough days, the price of his panic would have been one uncomfortable night.

What should you do with a similar problem? Hug a tree and develop a plan. Is there a road or river that you can reach? Will others begin a search for you? When will they start looking? Will they be able to find you? Do you have survival gear? How's the weather? Can you travel?

You have two options, wait for rescue or walk out. Don't make a decision if you're confused or frightened. Keep hugging that tree and stay put until you can think things through.
Look at the first option- wait. Usually it's better to sit tight. Walk out only if rescue is unlikely. If you are going to wait, you must do two things.

First, stay alive until rescue arrives. Build a shelter, gather food and water, and conserve your strength. Survival training and some equipment are useful now.

Second, make yourself easy to find. Light smoky fires using green vegetation during the day and bright fires at night. Use three fires arranged in a triangle. Three signals of any kind are a standard indication of distress.

Be ready to use a mirror to reflect sunlight toward a searching aircraft. No mirror? Then use shiny metal instead, perhaps a tin can or a knife blade. Use your hand as a preliminary target for the sun's reflection; then guide the sun's reflection towards the plane with the help of the spot on your hand.

Fabricate an abnormal terrain feature. Fashion a big circle in a clearing by walking in the snow or grass. Trampled grass or footprints in snow are obvious from the air. Make the circle about 10 feet wide and 60 feet in diameter. Piles of brush or burnt vegetation also makes a visible circle.

If a plane spots you, stand with legs apart and arms vertical. It's a standard ground-air signal that says "pick me up"; and identifies you as the victim.

Every 20 minutes or so, blow a whistle for three sets of three times each. It can be heard much farther than shouting by a ground search team and whistling is also easier than shouting.

The other option is travel and walk out on your own. If you first decided to wait for rescue and a week passes, the search may have been called off and you must consider walking out to survive. Have a destination or at least a direction to travel.

Don't start out blindly, you're lost not dumb. The old story about following a stream until it turns into a river, then following the river to civilization usually works.

But some streams flow into wilderness lakes and some rivers wind up at isolated spots on coast lines. Too bad you didn't look at a map before your trip. Following a waterway is difficult walking. It's better to observe the waterway from higher ground and follow it by looking from a distance.

Even without a compass, count on nature to provide directional information, but you must decipher it. The sun is your best indicator. Everyone knows the sunrises in the east and sets in the west. That's close, but not really true. The sun rises exactly in the east and sets exactly in the west only two days a year (on the first day of spring and the first day of fall). The actual direction of sunrise and sunset depends upon the date and latitude; it can be as much as 30 degrees away from east or west.

Determine direction from the sun in either of two ways. The first method is the most accurate and the slowest. Stand a two or three foot stick vertically in the ground. Mark the end of the shadow. Wait about 10 minutes and mark the end of the new shadow. Draw a line between the marks. The shadow has moved from the west to the east and the line is close to a true east-west indication.

A north-south line is right angles to this line. The east-west line is very accurate near noon and a little less so at other times.

The second method uses an analog watch. It's not as accurate, but it's fast and more suitable if you are moving.

Point the hour hand at the sun. Halfway between the hour hand and the number 12 on the watch is south. With a digital watch, try to visualize the hour hand.

Use the smallest angle between the hour hand and the number 12 except if it's more than six hours from noon. Then use the largest angle. If this is confusing, it becomes clear by determining direction using this method at about 6 AM or 6 PM.

Adjust your watch to show local suntime. If not set properly, using a watch to determine direction causes an error as high as 20 degrees. Determining the difference between your watch time and local suntime is easy. Use a vertical stick in the ground. Mark the end of the shadow every five minutes near noon. At local noon, the sun is highest in the sky and then, of course, its shadow is shortest. Change your watch to read 12 o'clock when the shadow is shortest. At local noon, the shadow is pointing directly north.

The moon and stars have limited usefulness to establish direction because night travel can be hazardous. You should be able to identify and use the North Star. Direction using the shadow of a full moon is determined the same way as with the sun.

If there's a crescent moon, draw an imaginary line connecting the tips of the moon. The line, extended to the horizon, points to the south.

At night, you might be able to see nightglow from any nearby cities. Use nightglow to establish your location.

OK, no compass, no watch, and it's cloudy. What then? Nature still provides more directional clues. You may have heard than moss grows on the north side of trees. It does, but it also grows on the south side and the east side and the west side. Moss on one tree is not a reliable directional indicator.

During some seasons, a reasonable directional indicator are the patches of snow on the north side of trees. Snow remains longer on the shady north side of trees and rocks.

A better indication, useable all year is tree growth. Branches on the south side of trees tend to grow horizontal while those on the north side tend to grow vertical. Don't trust an observation on one tree, study several. Tree growth depends on the sun, prevailing wind direction, nearby trees, injuries while growing, and other factors. So, you can't trust one tree to give an accurate indication. The best indicating trees grow alone in sheltered spots.

Because of the weight of their sun-seeking branches, dead trees tend to fall in a southerly direction. This indication is very crude and varies a lot because of wind, disease, other trees, and so on. But if you have nothing else, it's a start and can be a directional check as you travel in cloudy weather.

In some areas, ridges run east and west. Eons ago, the glaciers pushed debris along as they advanced and ridges were formed when they retreated. Again, one ridge isn't enough to establish direction. It helps to spend some time with a typographic map before your trip to determine terrain features.

Spiders tend to spin webs parallel with the prevailing wind; webs usually run east and west. Birds generally build nests in the lee of prevailing winds which is usually on the east side of trees. Migrating birds travel roughly north or south.

Now you can determine direction even without a compass. But it's easier and more accurate with a compass.

Leave a note at every campsite and at conspicuous spots as you travel. Include your name, date, and direction of travel to assist search parties. Add a notation that you're lost. Then anyone finding your note, part of a search team or not, will notify authorities. Also keep a diary of your travels; sketch a map showing landmarks and distance covered because it helps keep you on a direct course, logs progress, and allows you to retrace your path if necessary.

A small survival kit increases your chances tremendously. Always carry a knife, waterproof matches or a lighter, twine, space blanket, wire, a whistle, a mirror, a small flashlight, candles, fishing line, hooks, plus a pad and pencil. Everything fits in a small belt pouch.

In addition, you should normally carry a canteen, a map, a compass, and some food. Your clothing should be adequate for the coldest weather expected.

Mental attitude is a big factor in survival. Survivors tend to have certain traits. They're stubborn, determined, lead active lives and love both life and other people.

Acquire some survival skills now and prepare for the unexpected. Always carry a survival kit. Stay calm, hug that tree, and remember that survival is an attitude.

# Nature's Poetry

With their beautiful plumage and song, birds have been called the poetry of nature.

Bird watchers were among the first to become aware of the environmental crisis. You won't be alone – many others share this relaxing pastime. About 80 million Americans observe or feed them. Bird watching attracts both the meek and the macho.

And you'll have plenty of birds to watch; there are about one trillion birds worldwide with over a billion breeding in the United States. You can travel to foreign lands to enjoy birdwatching or stay in your backyard. Spend only a few minutes gazing out the kitchen window or spend your entire vacation looking for birds.

It's easy to start; the first thing to do is stop calling it bird watching. It's called birding by most enthusiasts.

Next, you should consider the purchase of a pair of binoculars and a guidebook. Neither is essential but both increase the pleasure and understanding of birding.

If you decide to purchase binoculars, here are some tips. Binoculars are characterized by two numbers, for example 7 and 50 (it's written as '7x50' but spoken as '7 by 50'). The first number is the magnification; the second is the diameter of the front lens in millimeters. A large diameter front lens allows a viewer to see better in dim light, but it also means a heavier pair of binoculars. Dim light observations are not essential to most birders.

A 7x50 pair of binoculars was the standard a few years ago, but 8x20 compact models are popular now. Most birders prefer compact binoculars because they're easier to carry and lighter to hold while viewing.

A few prefer 10x20 binoculars, but these, with their higher magnification, are harder to hold steady. To observe birds at long distances, consider a small telescope mounted on a tripod. This is useful for water birds because you can't approach them easily.

Binoculars cost up to several hundred dollars. Generally you get what you pay for, but
useable binoculars cost about $20. Shop around. If you wear glasses, buy binoculars with rubber cups on the eyepieces.

Guidebooks contain complete descriptions of birds with detailed drawings of plumage, description of their songs, and their normal range of habitat. The most popular pocket-sized guidebooks are <u>Birds of North America</u> and <u>A Field Guide to the Birds</u>. Local bookstores stock them.

Beginners tend to glance at an unfamiliar bird and then refer to the guidebook. With only a quick look, the small difference between some species prevents a definite identification. Study the bird until you're able to completely describe it. Look for other birds nearby because the males and females of some species have different plumage.

Compare its size to a common species (is it the size of a robin?), look for stripes or spots, observe the length and shape of the beak, and listen for its song. Does it hop or walk? Does it have an eye ring? Are the tail feathers rounded or forked? Note the terrain where you observed the bird. When you're satisfied that you've seen everything, only then refer to the guidebook. The identification process becomes easier and more reliable with practice.

Most birders keep a life list, which is a listing of all the species they've seen. The list can get long; there are about 8,700 species worldwide with about 840 in the United States. Some birders object to the importance that beginners place on the list. It adds an unnecessary sense of competition and beginners tend to ignore a species after it's on their life list. Bird habits are learned only after many observations and counting species is only a part of birding. Keep a life list, but recognize it's not a contest.

Most birds migrate, but some remain in the same area year-round. Migratory birds are seen only in the spring and fall and you'll see some species only in the summer, others only in the winter. Some birds vary their plumage between seasons. Because of these changes, birding is a four-season hobby.

Some birders arrange their vacations to observe specific species. They travel to the seashore, California or Florida because some birds have a very limited habitat range.

The Rocky Mountains roughly divide North American into "Eastern" and "Western" areas. Each region has a separate guidebook. Many birds are seen in both areas, but some are only seen in one region.

If travel is not for you, then try to attract birds to your yard and observe them from your kitchen window. Birders have seen 190 species from their window. In addition to being fun to watch, birds help control insects.

Invite them to your backyard by providing food, water, nesting areas and shelter. Specific foods attract different species. For example, offer thistle seed to lure finches, sunflower seeds for cardinals, blue jays, and nuthatches, raisins for robins and orioles, sugared water for hummingbirds, and suet for chickadees and woodpeckers.

Bird food can be expensive, but on a limited budget you can offer breadcrumbs and trimmed meat fat. Use a feeder because food on the ground attracts scavengers. Put up a birdfeeder and your first visitor will probably be a squirrel. They steal the food. Preventing the theft is difficult, but try wrapping thin metal around the post on a pole-mounted feeder or use a hanging feeder.

Another problem with feeders is cleanliness. If the food gets wet and becomes moldy, it spreads disease among the visitors. Bird droppings also spread disease. Periodically clean feeders and bird bathes with household bleach.

Many people feed birds in the winter but they ignore the need for grit to help digestion. If the ground is snow covered, place sand or crushed egg shells in the feeder for this purpose.

You can feed all year, but many people begin feeding only in the late fall. You should then continue feeding through the entire winter. Don't stop halfway because some experts say feeders draw birds from their natural habitat and they become dependent upon your food.

Birds feed at dusk during the winter to provide heat from metabolism to carry them through until morning. Birds really need high-energy suet or seeds to carry them through cold nights. Baked goods alone will not sustain them and you should provide more than bread in the winter. They may not survive even one night if your feeder is empty or has the wrong food.

Feeding into early spring encourages birds to nest nearby, but many people stop feeding as warm weather arrives because continued feeding tends to attract common sparrows and starlings. These then crowd out other species.

During warm weather, water attracts birds to your backyard. Ideally, an evergreen tree about 10 feet from your feeder or water supply helps to attract birds. If the tree is closer, birds fear predators are hiding there; if it's farther away, birds hesitate to approach because they can't easily evade a threat.

Attracting birds to your backyard can become an enormous endeavor. With feeders for different foods, heated water trays in winter, birdhouses and planted vegetation, your backyard can become a mini-sanctuary.

Birding complements other hobbies and activities. Hiking, boating, fishing, camping, and gardening are all enhanced by an interest in birds. Some birders make their own birdhouses and feeders; bird photography is a challenge to others; recording of bird songs is another aspect.

Eighty million birders can't be wrong. Watch the birds to learn about our world and enjoy Nature's Poetry.

# ARE YOU BUSY TONIGHT?

Long ago, humans feared the darkness. They believed ghosts, vampires, and all kinds of dangerous creatures appeared after sunset. People even believed the night air was unhealthy. Today we know better, but most of us retreat indoors at dusk. Perhaps some latent fear of the dark still remains. Young children are afraid of the dark, but will often overcome their fear if their parents accompany them on nighttime activities.

Night are longer in winter and shorter in summer, but over a year's time, every spot on Earth is in daylight an average of about 12 hours per day. Retreating indoors at dusk limits outdoor activities to only those 12 hours.

People have discovered two activities to enjoy at night. One of those, we can't even do during the day - stargazing. The other, night walking, is becoming popular because there are advantages to walking after sunset.

What are these advantages? First, fewer people. Next, during the summer, night walking is cooler. Then, in our busy lives, night is often the only opportunity to walk for exercise.

"The day has eyes; the night has ears," is an old Scottish proverb. During the day, our eyes provide most of our sensory input; at night, other senses become more important. Visual input is less at night, but new night walkers are surprised how much they still see.

It's easier to start night walking with a full moon because it's bright enough to instill confidence in even skeptics. Fall and winter provide the brightest moons because the moon rises higher during these seasons and is visible up to 12 hours each night. Moonlight reflecting off snow allow even better visibility. The moon, during spring and summer, travels a low trajectory; it's dimmer and is above the horizon for a shorter time.

Start night walking on city streets if you wish, but it's not the full experience. New sensations appear when walking along a trail or in a park. The night sounds different and smells different partly because you go outward and acquire sensory information rather than having visual information dumped on you as happens in daylight. Because it's so different, you return from night walking more alert and invigorated than after a day hike.

Sometimes, to overcome their initial misgivings, it helps a beginner to hike a trail first during the day and then hike it at night. Carry a flashlight and a whistle (to attract help) just in case. If you hike in a park, check with the park officials because some parks close at night and you could receive a ticket.

Stargazing is another nighttime activity, but many of us forget the night sky in our fast-paced lives. The night sky is masked by city lights and we're usually unable to clearly observe the heavens. You must travel away from urban areas to see the whole stellar display. Even away from city lights, a full moon interferes with viewing and the best time to observe the night sky is during a new moon. So you may hike during a full moon and, two weeks later, enjoy star gazing with a new moon.

A guidebook to the stars and heavens is desirable, but you don't need one at first. Everyone (well almost everyone) knows how to find Polaris, the North Star. Most of the guidebooks lead you to other constellations using Polaris and the Big Dipper as a reference point.

In winter, the constellation Orion the Hunter is another reference point to begin stargazing. Orion is identified by three bright stars that form his belt; the three stars are Alnitak, Alnilam, and Mintaka. The Great Nebula, which forms part of Orion's sword, appears as a fuzzy greenish star. Other stars in Orion are Betelgeuse, a giant red star, and Rigel, a blue-white giant. The colors are seen by some people with their naked eyes, but the colors become more vivid with binoculars.

Many star names are Arabic, because during the Dark Ages only Arabs looked at the heavens and we still use their definitions. As the Dark Ages ended, the Western World became more interested in the heavens. Because communication was so poor, everyone visualized different constellations and different names for them which caused much confusion. In 1930, an international group defined and named the present 88 constellations and established their precise boundaries.

During the summer, warmer weather and a dimmer moon allow a pleasant introduction to star gazing. During the summer, the Summer Triangle is visible. It's not a constellation, it's an easily discernible triangle formed by three bright stars, Deneb, Altair and Vega. Guidebooks use the Summer Triangle as another starting point to explore the summer sky.

Binoculars, or a monocular, are helpful. Both are described by two numbers (for example, 7 and 50) which seem to confuse some people. The numbers are often written 7x50 and spoken as '7 by 50'. The first number is the magnification; the second number is the diameter of the lens in millimeters. Don't purchase anything greater than ten magnification because a higher magnification is hard to hold steady without a tripod or other support. The larger the lens (the second number), the more light is gathered. To determine the suitability for star gazing, divide the larger number by the smaller number; the result should be bigger than the smaller number. For example, with 7x50 binoculars, divide 50 by 7 - the answer is a little more than 7 and so 7x50 binoculars are suitable for star gazing. Some inexpensive binoculars aren't aligned properly and you see double images. You can adapt to this problem for daytime viewing, but using defective binoculars at night is impossible. Try covering one eyepiece or use a monocular, if this is your problem.

Binoculars, or a telescope, allow a more complete examination of the heavens. You don't need them at first, because there are about 4,000 stars observable on a clear, dark night. But with binoculars, you will see galaxies, planets, nebulae, and many more stars.

Other nighttime displays are seen without binoculars. Your can watch meteor showers without binoculars. August and December are the best months; one shower peaks about August 12th, another peaks about December 14th. There are other meteor showers scattered throughout the year. The Northern Lights (Aurora Borealis) are caused by charged particles from the sun interacting with the earth's geomagnetic field. We usually think Northern Lights are most common in the winter, but they're actually spaced evenly all year.

If you live near a planetarium, ask about an introductory session for new explorers of the night sky. The planetarium store is a source for star maps and guidebooks for the heavens.

Your eyes need about 30 minutes to adjust completely to low light levels. To read a map or guidebook outdoors at night, use red light because it doesn't destroy the eye's sensitivity to low levels of illumination. Pilots, flying at night, use a red light to read their navigational books. Some flashlights come with a red lens or just cover any flashlight with red cellophane or red cloth.

Don't withdraw indoors when the sun sets. Enhance your life and your evenings by exploring the heavens or walking at night.

# THE CHANGING WILDERNESS

Can you imagine backpacking, or any other outdoor activity, without plastic or nylon?

Plastic bags and utensils are so common that most backpackers don't even think how great plastic is or what they would do without it. Nylon outdoor garments are ideal because of its toughness and ease of cleaning. Not too long ago, backpackers didn't have plastic or nylon.

Also not too long ago, the future of the wilderness didn't concern anyone because the wilderness was so vast and impervious to damage.

What was backpacking like without plastic, nylon, or any concern for the environment? What was backpacking like 40 or 50 years ago?

On a recent hike, something triggered memories of my first backpack and I realized how much backpacking has changed since then. My first backpack was in 1948, just after joining the Boy Scouts.

If you were to compare my gear then and our gear now, the first obvious difference is the pack. The packs were rucksacks; not much more than a canvas bag with straps. Nothing inside stayed dry during rainstorms.

Those that backpacked a lot acquired a pack-frame, which was a wood and metal assembly with ropes to secure a separate canvas bag, Its advantage over a rucksack was greater capacity (by using a larger canvas bag or two bags). Odd-shaped loads, like tent poles, tie onto a pack-frame easier than trying to load them into a rucksack. A pack frame probably was the grandparent of today's external frame packs. Everything still got wet. A few people had army surplus packs, which were no real improvement. None of the rucksacks had external pockets or waistbelts.

The rucksacks didn't have padded shoulder straps and shoulder discomfort was normal, I think we were trying to prove

81

we were real men. The lack of waistbelts added to the discomfort. We walked a lot with our hands under the straps to distribute the weight and reduce shoulder discomfort.

Sleeping gear has changed. One night on an early hike, a clicking noise woke me. Looking around with a flashlight, I saw a heap of quivering blankets nearby. The clicking was my companion's chattering teeth. Few people used sleeping bags, most slept in blanket rolls. Three wool blankets, arranged in interwoven layers, gave some padding underneath and some covering on top. Everything was held together with blanket pins (four-inch safety pins). The blankets were heavy to carry and not very warm. I remember only a few hikers using sleeping bags. Those few bags were made from cotton with kapok used as insulating filler and I think they cost about $10.

I don't remember anyone owning a sleeping pad. I don't think they even existed in 1948. Sleeping pads didn't exist, because they didn't have to. Cutting branches from evergreen trees and using them as a mattress was common practice. Not only was cutting branches allowed, the experienced backpackers encouraged it because it was so easy and "didn't do any harm."

No nylon tents, some heavy waterproof material (that may have been called oilcloth) was used in what we called mountain tents. The entrance was like a tunnel and didn't have zippers. It was closed by gathering it and tying it with a belt of material like a twist-tie. Zippers weren't very common 40 years ago, even the fly on men's pants were closed with buttons.

Those tents were a problem in the rain. To prevent ground water from seeping inside, we diverted the water away with trenches dug all around the outside. Some of us were overzealous and I bet some of those trenches are still there. Again, not only were trenches allowed, but they were encouraged as being the way smart backpackers did things.

A few hikers had heavy canvas pup tents waterproofed with paraffin. Waterproofing on those tents was mostly wishful thinking. During a rainstorm, a fine mist drifted down inside until the canvas absorbed water and swelled enough to seal the pores in the material. Touching the roof inside destroyed the surface tension at that spot and a leak started. The cure was to run a finger from the leak to the sidewall. The water followed the finger track and dripped at the edge of the tent instead of in the middle.

There weren't many casual clothes then. People had only dress clothes or work clothes. Most schools didn't even allow students to wear jeans. Adult scout leaders wore ties while backpacking. We occasionally met other adults while hiking. They were usually on day hikes and they wore ties.

Backpacking stoves didn't exist. We cooked using rocks or logs arranged to hold pots over the open fires. Campfires were started anywhere. Little concern was given to the scarring of rocks with fire.    Cutting down any convenient tree for firewood was common and a big roaring fire was the trademark of a good camp. We made sure the fire was extinguished before departure, but never tried to scatter the ashes or anything.

Most of our food was canned, no freeze-dried food. Home freezers 40 years ago were tiny compartments in refrigerators and no one could bring frozen foods for the first meals on backpacks. We ate a lot of canned beans and pancakes. Lunch was usually peanut butter and jelly sandwiches. If we ate meat, it was canned. The younger hikers liked Spam, but our scout leaders, mostly veterans of World War II, refused to eat Spam because it was so common in army rations and they said they had enough of it for a lifetime.

The only powdered drink I remember was Kool-Aid and I think that was newly introduced. No instant coffee either.

We cushioned eggs by packing them with dry cereal together in jars (glass jars of course). They usually survived.

Water never was a problem. We dipped water from streams and lakes at random. We occasionally treated water that looked murkier than usual with Halazone tablets. We never heard of Giardia.

No one carried trash out. We knew the cans would rust away in a few years and the paper would also deteriorate. We felt we did the right thing by placing our trash in a heap 100 feet or so away from the tent sites instead of randomly throwing it into the woods.

Never dug a hole for body waste. Again, we felt we did the right thing by stepping 20 feet off the trail.

The only flashlights we carried used D-cell batteries. We used these large batteries because smaller batteries (like AA size) didn't have much capacity. Only zinc-carbon batteries were available and it didn't seem to matter if you used the flashlight or not, the batteries just didn't last long.

No one took photographs because cameras were bulky; they were appropriately called "box cameras." Of course, no radios.

This was after World War II and military surplus gear was common. We felt the army gear was the "real stuff." Most hikers wore shoes instead of hiking boots; a few wore hi-top sneakers.

Few people then had cars and even fewer had two cars. Usually we took buses and trains to the trailheads lugging the packs and all. Public transportation seemed easier and certainly more common then.

We seldom met other backpackers. When we did, they were usually teenagers like us. I suppose that with the longer workweek and less convenient transportation, adults didn't have much chance to enjoy the wilderness. Never, never saw women on the trail. Women didn't participate in many outdoor activities then. Those activities were probably considered too macho.

Many of the older men I backpack with now are former Boy Scouts. The love of the outdoors remained and we now are inviting others to join us. Wives, children, grandchildren, and friends are in step with these former Boy Scouts. Hiking groups today are mixed, with a wide-age range, a broad spectrum of occupations, and a high percentage of women. Today's hiking groups are one-third to one-half female.

There's a trend among backpackers. It's a tendency to take hi-tech gear into the wilderness. Companions on recent hikes have carried pocket navigational computers and radios. I've heard of people carrying cell-phones and even a TV set into the wilderness. There's some advantage to having a phone or navigational computer (in case of emergency), but it's not the wilderness anymore.

The wilderness has changed since my first backpack in 1948. There's less of it and what's left is in danger from overuse and pollution. We felt then that the wilderness would always be there and we didn't really have to take care of it. Concern for the environment is relatively recent and has occurred only since we discovered how much damage we're doing. What was common practice years ago, cutting branches and huge fires and everything, is inexcusable behavior today. No real backpacker today would cut a tree down or build a fire outside a firepit or discard trash randomly. We hope today's backpacker might say something like, "I want to preserve our wilderness for the future."

# POSTSCRIPT

Today's young people are very involved with TV, computers and other electronic devices. As a result, their physical condition is not all it should be. Make an attempt to introduce them to the outdoors. Their body and mind will improve and hopefully these young people will understand your effort.

# ABOUT THE AUTHOR

Roger Meyer is a Michigan based writer and specializes in writing articles on the outdoors and World War II. His 200 published magazine articles have appeared in over 80 publications. This is his sixth book. He's a retired Air Force officer and a retired electronic engineer.